The
SEVEN LEVELS
OF TRUTH

The Answer to Life's Biggest Question

BILL HEINRICH

"Powerful and Transformational, astrologically speaking Bill Heinrich's scorpio energy has a laser focus on teaching us about our individual purpose and power!"

— **Michael O'Connor**, *Humanistic Astrologer, Sunstar Astrology*

"You have all the questions inside you and this book has all the answers."

— **Jose Miguel Ruiz**, *New York Times Best Selling Author The Fifth Agreement*

"Bill is a powerful speaker with a very persuasive message and now you can take this transformative message home and follow the blueprint to your life purpose!"

— **Dave Vanhoos,** *Speaking Empire*

"A direct path to your True Life Purpose, this book is a must read for anyone that wants to make a difference in the world."

— **Peter Anthony**, *You Will Change The World*

This book is about awareness and choice!
Take off your blindfold, eliminate blind spots and
perpetuating negative beliefs. By creating awareness
in life you can make powerful choices and live a
fully authentic, purposeful and fulfilling life.

This book for is for anyone seeking answers,
solutions, or true success in life.
Our birth-rite is abundance, love, peace and joy.
The Seven Levels of Truth will allow you
to achieve all of these results in your life.

Learn more at TrueLifePurposeNow.com

CONTENTS

PREFACE

For nearly 25 years I have been focused on my personal transformation. My journey has been a long slow process with an emphasis
on identifying resources that would make my life peaceful, meaningful
and simpler. I have learned many new ways to perceive life and live
with less struggle. The information I uncovered led me to believe I had
found secret resources that I had no awareness of previously during my
struggles with life. How sad that so many people struggle and there is a
multitude of free resources available for everyone that create a simple
life and eliminate stress and overwhelm. It is almost baffling to me that
these resources are not part of our basic education.

As I learned about these resources, I kept thinking about how
many people could use this information to improve their lives, regardless of their current situation. I was determined to find a way to make
this information available to others in a manner that they could understand, which will allow anyone to start a new path of peace, joy,
and freedom. I started doing research and proof of concept testing to
accumulate data to support my discovery. I intend to provide you with
the information in a simple yet effective format, realizing that making
the information easy to digest with simple guidelines will support your
accelerated transformation.

I have spent the last six years coaching people on how to change their lives and live a more powerful, grateful and abundant life. The results have been astounding! When you understand who you are, what gifts you have to share and the lessons you are here to learn, you have a blueprint for living life. All of my clients made significant life changes, and more importantly, they got results instantly. What if you could live your most powerful life? How would that look? How would that feel? How do you envision the power you can access? What outcome does power give you? Breathe in and feel your power, and sit with it for a moment. How does it feel?

I had a different point of view regarding power before I was able to understand what power is, how to use it, and how to get the best results. Imagine having a blueprint to create a powerful life, a plan specifically designed for you. Imagine having total control over your life and living in a continuously calm, peaceful and abundant environment. I created a blueprint developed from my spiritual DNA; it is simple, clear and compelling. You can create a design also by following the guidelines in this book. I have developed a "recipe" (so to speak) from my research that you can use if you choose. The ingredients are yours to use as you please because we are each on a different path.

The exciting part is that you get to determine how the recipe gets put together; I give you all of the ingredients, and you make the "cake"! You can't make it incorrectly. Whatever you do will work, and with each choice you make you will learn how to improve the recipe. The ingredients are the same for everyone, but the quantities of the ingredients vary from one person to the next. You will experience a new awareness that instantly changes how you view your place in life and will learn how to make choices that allow you to live more powerfully! You will start to remember what you forgot to remember and instantly begin making new choices that bring purpose, passion, and prosperity to your life.

Along the path of life we received guidance on how to live life and some of that information no longer serves us today. It was great at the time, and it has served its purpose, but we each have many internal beliefs that no longer support us. I promise you that you will learn about all of the components that are required to live a fulfilling, purposeful life. Your part is a willingness to have an open-mind and explore how to apply these resources in your life each day. Then you can determine what best serves you. If you are reading this and defending how you live life, you will get minimal benefits from this book. I intend to show you new resources you can apply in your life each day. Whatever you choose will be perfect for you. Life is where we get to exercise our greatest gift; free will and choice.

My inspiration and motivation are to share with others these powerful resources because much of the turmoil in the world today is caused by misdirection in our lives. Living life without any direction is not a statement that most people are willing to accept. But I have found this to be true - most people are making decisions based on who they aren't!. People are making decisions about life based on information that is in direct resistance to who they are and this can only create challenges, stress, overwhelm and frustration in anyone's life. It has been true for everyone that I have encountered.

Every person I have worked with agreed 100% with the fact they were making decisions with wrong information and their life was effectively out of control. The evidence has been overwhelming, and when they made a new choice using my Blueprint the results were immediate. You will experience the same. After reading "The Seven Levels of Truth" you get to determine if these resources will be of any benefit to you; it is your choice. I want you to use this information in your life, as you see fit. I am not here to convince you, nor am I interested in a debate; I am only sharing what I have learned, taught others, and witnessed miraculous results. Use what you like and discard the remainder, after all you get to choose how you will experience life.

I have known I was going to write this book for a long time. I had the outline, title, and purpose but I didn't have the material necessary to make sure that you would understand the information and be able to apply it in your life. I also had to overcome the voices in my head that were saying "What do you know?" "How will people react to this book?" "How could I have anything of value to share?" Who are you to share the Answer to Life's Biggest Question?" It has ignited my feelings of inadequacy which continually created writing blocks. It feels awkward to be exposing myself; after all, I am not a writer by my own admission.

My Divine Purpose is to share my knowledge with others through the written and spoken word. By writing this book, I am fulfilling my purpose. I am taking actions fueled by my life purpose. I remain detached from the results, knowing that this book will improve someone's life and hopefully it is your life! Today in the coaching industry the "new" business card is a book. It seems as if everyone is writing a book and I am not a "me too" kind of person. I don't follow the crowd. I am not writing this book to "be seen" or gain credibility or fame. I intend to share with you resources that will show you a straightforward way to live a very fulfilling life. You will come to understand after gaining more awareness of the resources available that we each have a specific life purpose. As you access these resources your perception of life will take on a new meaning.

Writing this book has been a long and exciting journey. It has taken four years of research, patience, and reverence to get to the point of publishing the book. You will learn as you read the "Seven Levels of Truth" that all of these resources are simple to access and the results you achieve by using these tools in your life will be profound. Each day I use these resources and my life continues to improve, and my clarity of purpose gets expressed more powerfully. Regardless of your path in life, your religious or spiritual beliefs, and current situation, this information will support your choices and improve your life. The only pre-requisite is an open mind. There is nothing more frustrating than being in resistance to your life purpose without any awareness on your part. It is how we believe life should be because we don't know any another way. You will also come to learn that there is nothing more gratifying than living your true life purpose.

I haven't done this alone. Over the years I have learned about these resources from some very evolved holistic practitioners. They have contributed different pieces of the materials and resources I share with you. One of the most interesting parts of the journey is understanding that holistic practitioners always adds something of value from their personal experience into their teachings. My personal touch has been developing a Blueprint to follow that I guarantee will work, if you follow the guidelines.

I would like to recognize Andrrea Hess, spiritual teacher, who introduced me to my Divine Gifts. When I was made aware of my Divine Gifts, it activated an internal awareness and knowledge that I possessed and I have been working with them ever since. Other people that have made this book possible are Michael O'Connor, Humanistic Astrologer who informed me of the importance of getting this book published and assisted me in the editing of "The Seven Levels of Truth". Joe Frazzette, the author of "Secrets of the Hypnotic Formula", assisted me with the title. A. D. Cook, nationally known artist, speaker, designer and author of "Dream to Launch," created the cover and designed the layout of the book.

Some of my favorite authors that have influenced me are Gary Zukav, "The Seat of The Soul", Dan Millman, "The Life You Were Born to Live", Deepak Chopra, "The Seven Spiritual Laws of Success", I reference these three books at least once a month. The other books on my bookshelf are "The Power of Now", Eckhart Tolle, "Power vs. Force", David Hawkins, "Change Your Thoughts Change Your Life", Wayne Dyer, and "Ask And It Is Given", Esther and Jerry Hicks. These are the books that teach "pure truth" in one form or another. The most important book, in my opinion, is "The Life You Were Born To Live" because this points out the different aspects of our life lessons. Knowing where problem areas are can smooth out the journey. We are always changing and growing creating new lessons to learn.

This book is named The Seven Levels of Truth" because we each have the same seven Divine Gifts but the proportions of each gift are different in every person; no two people are the same. When we use all seven gifts in the manner intended it creates our Authentic Self Expression and our truth expressed in the world. When we are unaware of our Divine Gifts, our ultimate individual truth is blocked, and we struggle with our daily life. "The Seven Levels of Truth" are seven Divine Gifts that we each have and each Divine Gift has its own level energy with its own specific purpose. When we combine the proper proportions of these energies into our life, the results are beyond your ability to imagine in this moment.

If you sincerely desire to live a purposeful life, you will find all the ingredients necessary in this book. There is no need to search any longer "outside" of yourself, as all of the answers you seek are "inside" you. You have the opportunity to experience sharing your unique gifts with the world and I assure you that there is nothing more gratifying in life. Living your true life purpose and sharing your authentic self-expression with the world is a gift beyond measure. I look forward to having you join me and countless others that have found their authentic path in life.

Author's note: I make reference to "self-actualization" and our "true life purpose" throughout the book. Although self-actualization and our true life purpose are quite similar in nature, they each have a different basis of understanding, perception and individual expression. Self-actualization is the journey to achieving human potential (from a physical perspective of life). Living your true life purpose and your authentic self-expression are energetic values that you infuse into your life. Consequently, our true life purpose is self-actualization significantly enhanced with our Divine Gifts and the energy of our true life purpose.

www.soulrealignment.com

www.sunstarastrology.com

www.joefrazzette.com

www.adcookdesign.com & www.dreamtolaunch.com

CHAPTER ONE ~ Introduction

The catalyst for change in anyone's life is unwillingness. We are unwilling to live a certain way any longer, and we start to make choices that will eliminate the discomfort we feel. That was the case for me on a cold winter night in Lake Tahoe more than 20 years ago. I lost control of my temper, and my anger got the best of me, again. In a split second, I went from peaceful to angry, headed towards rage! But something happened as the anger started to build. I had a moment of clarity, and I realized that I was literally out of control. As the anger began to turn into a rage, a voice inside me said: "Bill, this isn't you." I heard the voice very clearly, loud enough for me stop, step back and pause. The voice was so powerful that it got my attention and created a moment of clarity. It may have been an out of body experience with the clarity I had in the midst of anger and rage. At that moment I was shown the comparison between myself in the moment and my Divine Self.

At the time, I didn't realize what I had experienced, but I knew that I had to go find out why I was so miserable. It was as if I had no choice! I went downstairs and told the woman that I was in a relationship with that I was so miserable that I couldn't stand it a moment longer and I had to go find out why. I walked out the front door and never came back. I didn't know what I was going to do, but I knew I had to make drastic changes in my life. I trusted that I would be guided to the answers. I was committed to learning why life was so challenging and confusing to me. My transformation has been a very long and evolving process; a daily journey of self-discovery. My primary focus since that moment has been learning how to live more peacefully, joyfully and abundantly.

The story of my life in transformation (which continues today) is exciting, but that isn't the purpose of this book. I want to share with you the Blueprint that I have developed over the past 20 years. I have discovered the secret to life's biggest question: how to live a purposeful life, feeling self-fulfilled and living your life purpose! I know this sounds like quite a claim, but it's true! I have used this Blueprint with hundreds of people successfully. That's why I am writing this book, to share everything I have learned with you. Throughout the book I will be sharing some of my experiences during my transformation, and it's been a fascinating journey. But I'm writing this book to share with the world the ingredients needed for you to live your true life purpose. I have found the answer! Everything I share with you in this book is the "best of the best" that I have discovered and implemented in my life.

Although the story of my transformation might make an interesting book, I have no interest in writing about that at this time. I only want to share with you the resources that will make a miraculous difference in your life instantly. The most direct path between two places is a straight line. That is the path I will follow in this book showing you the five ingredients necessary to live your true life purpose. The only thing in life that will bring you a sense of authentic personal fulfillment is living your life purpose. Everything else falls short, providing momentary happiness which over time turns into that feeling of "there has to be more to life."

Do you experience stress and overwhelm in your life? Why do you want to change? Are you trying to get away from discomfort and pain? Are you just curious? Maybe you are a seeker, are already self-actualized and want to live at a higher vibration. Do you feel like there might be more to life? Perhaps, you feel like something is missing and there's no sense of fulfillment. All of the clients I have worked with have felt that way, like something was missing. They were right! What was missing was their authentic self-expression. If this is the case, you are part of my tribe; we know that we have more to offer and we want to make a difference in the world. We want to (quietly) leave a legacy.

Are you wanting to experience living an authentic life? Whatever has motivated you to read this book is perfect for you! We are unique, and we each have had experiences that are different. We may have experienced the same type of problem in our life, but our perception of it is going to be completely different. Most people that I encounter have a burning passion that they are unable to satisfy because they are locked down in day-to-day survival. This book will give you all the resources needed to live an authentic life with passion, purpose, and prosperity. As you read this book, please keep in mind that how you use these tools is your choice and whatever you choose for you will be perfect.

These are the five different resources that I am going to share with you; Understanding our needs, your Divine Gifts, your Life Lessons, Transcendence, and physical and non-physical resources that will accelerate or block your journey to self-fulfillment. We will go through each of these areas thoroughly enough for you to see how they affect your life. We each have our specific life path; and no two people are the same. This isn't a "one size fits all" and you get to choose. There are different ways to implement these resources in your life. You must select which feels best for you at the time, and you will intuitively know the choice to make. The irony of what I have discovered is the simplicity required to live your life purpose. You will find that when life is complicated, you're moving in the wrong direction. Living a thoroughly self-actualized life is quite simple, and it allows you to experience life to its fullest. Are you familiar with the term self-actualization?

Abraham Maslow spent years researching how people could achieve peak potential, which he calls self-actualization. Maslow created the "Hierarchy of Needs" which describes the different levels of human needs, culminating with self-actualization. I have been researching and studying self-actualization for the past 25 years from a non-physical perspective. Maslow's research has been from a physical perspective. I have continually searched for new ideas, perceptions, and concepts that would lead me towards a more fulfilling life. My research, studies, and exploration took me down a different path, and I didn't discover Maslow's "Hierarchy of Needs" until just recently.

I was looking for a way to share what I have learned in a way everyone would understand and start to apply these resources in their life. Maslow's "Hierarchy of Needs" is what I was searching for because we all understand basic survival instincts that fill our needs, and Maslow provides us with a solid foundation to reference. You will soon learn that our needs are misunderstood and our desires to fulfill them are blocking us from our life purpose. We must understand each of the individual levels of needs and how they interact. This knowledge will allow us to live a more self-actualized life. Isn't that what you desire? Or maybe you are looking for a way to end the struggle and misery of what you call a day-to-day life. That was my motivation - misery. What is your motivation?

The direction of my transformational path led me to start meditating and learning to sit quietly. There was so much noise and chaos in my life that I wanted to experience peacefulness. Meditation opened a whole new world to me in the non-physical realm. Not only did I find peacefulness while meditating, but I also started to notice some clarity. I quickly realized that there are resources available to us in the non-physical form that enhance our lives in the physical. As I explored, I found the information fascinating! This is what led to me start studying metaphysics because I recognized that experiencing the non-physical realm through meditation brought new perceptions into my life, and everything began to change. When I applied the non-physical resources into my physical world, there was an immediate improvement in my life. Our potential, I learned quickly, can only be accessed through the non-physical realm. This is what Maslow calls transcendence.

A majority of my research and study has been in the area of metaphysics, and now I have come full circle back to the physical world and Abraham Maslow's "Hierarchy of Needs." Abraham Maslow studied human potential; his motivation was focusing on what he called "Peak Potential." Maslow creates a wonderful path for us to follow starting with our most basic needs. This book is a blueprint for you to follow that will create a journey to self-actualization, and your true life purpose. The difference between self-actualization and living your true life purpose is a simple matter of perception. Maslow's approach is from a perspective of living in the physical and adequately fulfilling our needs which leads us to self-actualization.

My perspective is from living my true life purpose with an energetic perspective. I show you how to transcend your life from the non-physical. I will share all of my resources and also show you how we get blocked from them. Maslow's research indicated that it was necessary to learn to transcend your perspective to achieve self-actualization. If you are struggling to understand or don't grasp these concepts, don't be concerned. Everything is going to be thoroughly explained; that's the purpose of this book.

You will achieve self-actualization by reading this book. I guarantee it! Self-actualization speaks to your journey, not the destination, and your ability to remain open-minded for the sole purpose of your personal growth. If you're reading this book, you are self-actualized! You have a curiosity that needs to be satisfied, and you desire to find additional tools that will enrich your life further. You will find many tools and resources in this book that will serve you very well in your self-actualized life. This book is a blueprint for you to follow that will continually enhance your journey to self-actualization and lead you to your true life purpose. You will find critical components that are the essential guidelines and when acknowledged, take you immediately to a higher level of self-actualization. It is as simple as understanding which steps in this blueprint will provide the most significant benefit to your current situation, and making a choice. Self-actualization is achieved through a deeper understanding of your inner-game. Your perceptions, beliefs, obligations and stories are what create your inner-game.

I am a "High Level" business coach, and I have been working directly with clients (around the world) doing one-on-one and group coaching using these resources for over five years. I offer all of my clients a 100% money back guarantee if they aren't successful and no one has ever requested a refund. When you examine the process, you will remember what you forgot to remember; we are spiritual beings having a human experience. We have a natural internal instinct that compels us to pursue self-actualization. I believe that the misery we experience in life comes from an internal knowing that we are not pursuing our intended purpose in life. Once you get connected to this path, there is no turning back! We wouldn't settle for anything less than achieving a higher level of self-actualization each day. Each day we have the opportunity to learn more, about life, about self-actualization and how to make our most significant contribution and fulfill our true life purpose. Each breath, each thought and each action we take determines our level of success. But we must understand our needs to make choices that enhance our results and our life. The "inner-game" holds all of the answers because our inner beliefs, stories, and our logic all support a life that is focused on satisfying your physical needs.

Abraham Maslow's book "Motivation and Personality" was written to focus on the positive is was only focusing on what was wrong with us and what we needed to fix and Abraham Maslow was only interested in our human potential, not what was wrong with us. Maslow developed the "Hierarchy of Needs" which explains the different levels (areas) of needs that we experience in life.

Maslow's "Hierarchy of Needs"

Physiological Needs

Air, food, water, shelter

Safety Needs

Physical. financial, emotional (all areas of life)

Love and Belonging Needs

Friendship, intimacy, trust, and acceptance

Esteem Needs

Self-acknowledgment and respect

Self Actualization Needs

Reaching full human potential

Maslow's "Hierarchy of Needs" prioritizes our needs from the most basic level up to self-actualization. As we experience our needs, we integrate self-actualization into different aspects of our life. However, before we can integrate self-actualization in our lives, we need to understand our attachment to getting our physical desires fulfilled. Our perceptions of life are through the eyes of our physical needs, and they have us trapped in survival mode. Everyone is controlling each other because we each have an agenda and live competitively. We are always trying to increase our level of survival in life by adding more of life's physical comforts. Our focus, and society's focus in general, is based on consumption of material goods and we remain alert looking for the latest trend or fashion. As a society we are lost. There is so much more to life when you become self-actualized and live your true life purpose. It is easy to get stuck living in survival mode without any visible path that will take us to self-actualization. We look for answers outside of ourselves, and all the answers are sitting inside you.

"What is necessary to change a person is to change his awareness of himself."

— *Abraham Maslow*

Survival is a theme in life, and there are millions of different ways that fear is created based on perceptions that are anchored in survival. This is when you start to feel life get overwhelming; there seems to be no way out. When we have a survival mindset, we are always in the state of competing to survive. We judge ourselves as "winners" or "losers." Everywhere around us are facts that support the existence of competitive survival and a belief that money will solve our problems. What's happening outside of us is how we focus on life, rather than how we feel on the inside. We are allowing our circumstances to dictate the outcome of our life because we do not have the internal awareness that would enable us to create our own lives differently. You have all the answers; you simply need awareness of which pieces are going to make a difference. You have an inner knowledge that allows you to create new perceptions that result in your ability to transform your life.

You have all the answers inside you; only awareness will show you which pieces are going to make a difference. Awareness is the answer! We are living in the school of survival; everyone's focus is on survival. We are taught how to "fit in" to society. We are focusing on surviving rather than concentrating on thriving. To move from a state of survival, we need to understand all of the resources available. Life is magical and precious, and we realize this intellectually, but we don't support this belief with our thoughts, words, and actions each day by making life more magical and precious. Why? Because we live in a self-policing society that only concentrates on survival. Our focus is on making more money because that creates a more comfortable level of survival.

When I became aware of Abraham Maslow and his "Hierarchy of Needs" I became filled with excitement. As I was reviewing the different levels of the needs; it was obvious to me how we get lost in life chasing survival. When we look at the "Hierarchy of Needs" individually, we will realize that they are all intertwined in our life experiences. We get stuck in the lower levels of satisfying our needs. The biggest dis-ease in life is the M and M disease.....Me and More! This is where I lived trying to fill needs that have a never-ending appetite!

To transcend your life, you must have some knowledge of metaphysics. Whenever I speak openly about metaphysics, the naysayers are quick to render negative opinions or criticize what is referred to as the "new age" lifestyle. People have formed judgments about metaphysics because it's non-physical and not understood. Metaphysics appears to be threatening to a life of survival because it is the exact opposite! Living in survival keeps you attached to feeling safe, and a familiar repetitive life. Anything unknown is threatening to life as you know it. Anything unknown is threatening to what is known in your life because survival is about defending and protecting; that is how you survive! You are getting this information from someone that was an expert at survival. I was a chameleon while living in survival. I became what I needed to be to make others happy so I could get what I wanted. Being consumed with survival only increased my level of misery and each day life became more baffling and confusing.

When you start to venture into the non-physical universe, you will quickly realize that "home is where your heart is" and your heart (solar plexus) is your non-physical command center. Your heart speaks only truth, and that truth is in the form of feelings. Not only is metaphysics a vital part of our lives, but it is also an integral part of our life. Our perceptions got skewed due to our survival mentality; we look at everything from the physical to protect our level of comfort. Improving our level of comfort and happiness is the goal of survival! Nothing matters other than our physical life on earth. We get caught in a very narrow, linear path that is called life, and we are taught to and expected to "fit in." The moment that we do something that is beyond the boundaries of a survival lifestyle we get challenged by others for "getting out of the box." Sound familiar? Everyone refers to "outside the box" as a way to grow but what is the box? The box is constructed solely by others opinions of how your life should be lived!

As you gain more knowledge about energy, you will become familiar with how energy flows. Energy is a vibration and energy is the language of the heart. Emotions (energy in motion) are the energy that is most closely associated with the heart. When you learn to create energy that connects with the higher vibrational energy of the universe you can transcend any situation, instantly! When we consciously create energy to transcend our life, it will always be received by another person's heart, whether they are aware of it or not. If you are fearful, they will feel fear and react fearfully! A loving perspective no matter how difficult the conversation, will filter through to the other person and they will feel your loving energy. The person you're speaking to will hear the words intellectually using their mind.

But they will "feel" the energy behind your words. Now that we understand that everything is vibration, you achieve self-actualization by raising your vibration. At the most fundamental level of life, there are only two emotions: love and fear. What is the energy generated by these two emotions? Which one supports survival? Love is what will allow you to move towards self-actualization. When we are fearful what energy are we creating? Like-attracts-Like! You can alter any situation by transcending the energy! It only requires awareness and choice.

As I studied metaphysics, I discovered that we are part of a universe that is so immense it goes to infinity! No one knows for certain where we came from or where we are going. Oh, there are plenty of opinions about this topic depending on whom you ask! Here is what I have found out through my research: we live on earth and are a minuscule portion of the universe, but we live life as if we are the center of the universe! Nothing matters other than our physical life on earth. We must live our lives in alignment with the laws that run the universe, or if not we will be living in resistance, not in the flow. Our vibration determines what universal resources we can connect with and utilize to stop surviving and start thriving.

Understanding metaphysics is crucial to self-actualization because it is necessary to transcend your experiences to make them beneficial for all involved. If you are living in survival, this may seem a bit confusing. When we open ourselves to other resources that will enhance our lives, we need to look no further than the operating instructions for the universe. The universe operates on some elementary principles, and we'll look at these principles later in the book so that you'll gain an in-depth understanding and be able to apply them to your life on a daily basis. As we change our energy, we transform our lives; this is how you thrive. These universal principles are not accessible to survival energy because survival energy is rooted in limiting beliefs. You can't be self-actualized and live a survival lifestyle; they do not mix.

> **"Transcendence refers to the very highest and most inclusive or holistic levels of human consciousness, behaving and relating, as ends rather than means, to oneself, to significant others, to human beings in general, to other species, to nature, and to the cosmos."**
>
> — *Abraham Maslow*

Having the option to choose love (thriving) instead of fear (surviving) will change your life. Even if you reacted to a situation with fear and created more chaos, worry and stress, you can change the situation instantly when you come from a place of love. It is all about the energy we are creating; this is what allows us to connect with the energy of the universe. The universe only responds to energy; it doesn't use thought or logic. The universe doesn't discuss the merits of a given situation or desire. It merely responds to energy.

The dictionary defines transcendence as existence or experience beyond the normal or physical level. As Abraham Maslow shows us, transcendence is the most important part of self-actualization, and it must be integrated into our lives to achieve self-actualization and live your true life purpose. As we go through the Hierarchy of Needs from physiological, to safety, to love and belonging, esteem and then self-actualization, it's easy to see that we're here on earth to be of service to others. Sharing our magnificence, our unique gift with the world, is how we create a life of passion, purpose, and meaning.

We each came to earth with unique gifts to share. Have you ever heard that? We are like snowflakes; no two are the same! Through my personal transformation experience over the last 20+ years, I have found that both of these statements are true. I realized very early on in my transformation that metaphysics was the key to success. I kept getting introduced to various ways to improve my life, and they were all directly connected to metaphysics and universal energy. I took the safe road and continued to explore, but I didn't tell anyone because metaphysics was an area that always seemed to get criticized by others. I am always looking for new information that will allow me to live a more actualized and powerful life. As I studied metaphysics, I became more familiar and comfortable with my intuition and my sensitivity to energy.

Age, ethnicity, geographic location, level of success and your financial condition will never determine your self-actualization. The resources I share here are free! Everyone in the world has access to them. The only requirement is an open mind and the desire to live a purposeful life. You'll come to understand how powerful these resources are and how to implement them in your life. It is also essential to understand what is blocking you, standing in your way or holding you back from living a self-actualized life. Life is about lessons; in fact, good mental health is your ability to get past your current problem with the understanding that another challenge is waiting to appear. This is the nature of life, and the emotional manner in which you handle these challenges determines your quality of life. If you choose to live a conscious life it requires personal responsibility and awareness as the key ingredients. The more knowledge you have, the more choices you have. Free will and choice are our most valuable assets. When your options are limited, you are limited and you become a victim of circumstances. Victims give away their power, and self-actualized people express their power!

There are many different types of energy, and the most powerful energy available to us is the energy of our Divine Gifts. We each come to earth with seven Divine Gifts: Divine Compassion, Divine Creation, Divine Order, Divine Healing, Divine Self Expression, Divine Truth and Divine Power. We each have the same seven Divine Gifts, but we have them in different proportions. Each of us has our own unique energetic spiritual DNA. It is the energetic expression of these Divine Gifts that create our true life purpose. Our authentic self-expression is our highest form of self-actualization. Everyone I speak with about living their true life purpose believes that their occupation is what defines their purpose and that is not true! It isn't what you do; it is the energy you flow into your life. We are so attached to the physical that we are defined by what others see, not who we are (on the inside). One must understand the difference between the physical (what you see each day) and the non-physical which is the energy we create to fuel our thoughts, words, and actions. You will realize how vital your energy is to you and the rest of the world.

"The two most important days in your life are the day you were born and the day you find out why."

— *Mark Twain*

The most significant challenge that all of the people I have worked with experienced is an absence of clarity. They didn't understand how life works because their daily lives are focused on survival and everyone around them is living in survival. Once I showed them all of the pieces and clicked all of the puzzle pieces together for them, their lives change instantly! They realized that during their life they had learned survival techniques from their caregivers. As they attempted to move up through the Hierarchy of Needs, they are continually blocked from growth because of some of their beliefs about survival. How can you improve your life when you don't understand how life works? There are millions of moving parts to life, and when you don't know how it works, it is impossible to make choices that allow living a more fulfilling life. There are too many pieces, and it gets very complicated!

I have spent the last six years in coaching doing research and "proof of concept" as I worked directly with clients. Five things remained consistent with everyone I worked with:

1. Everyone had an internal belief that there was more to life than just making a living. (They felt as if something was missing!)

2. Everyone had a sincere desire to live a life of meaning and purpose.

3. Everyone wants to contribute to the world in a way that will make a significant difference.

4. Everyone felt frustrated by the results they were getting for the amount of spiritual work they had done.

5. Everyone agreed it was as if they were living life with a blindfold on!

I will show you how to live a more fulfilling, purposeful life using the resources in this book. That is my promise to you. Your results will be determined by the choices you make, moment by moment, every day. You don't need to learn to be self-actualized! You only need to become aware of what is blocking you, standing in your way or holding you back from living your true life purpose. When you clear away the blocks, you are allowing more life force energy to flow, and that will take you directly to self-actualization and living your true life purpose. People love being responsible (rather than accountable) for the lives they create when they're living with purpose and passion. At the moment you see all of the pieces of the puzzle click together you immediately become responsible and start creating the life of your dreams. This is not complicated; it is effortless. You only need the blueprint.

Living a life of survival is exhausting and complicated, and it leaves us frustrated, stressed and defeated. The rules of survival get changed moment by moment by others (typically to benefit their survival). The golden rule in survival is this: He/she with the most gold makes the rules! The life of survival only contaminates you with negative energy. We are continually having to adjust our life, attempt to understand what is happening and trying to make the best decisions for a future that is out of our control.

We got misled along the path of life and some of the things we learned no longer serve us in our lives today. You know what choices to make, as long as you understand the right resources and follow the operating instructions. *Let's get started.*

Guideposts to Expand Your Journey:

1. What do you feel is missing in your life today?

2. What do you desire to create in your life?

3. What are three things standing in your way or blocking you?

CHAPTER TWO ~ The Hierarchy of Needs

Imagine waking up in the morning without a care in the world and all of your needs are satisfied. You have no stress; your life is full of bliss. Wouldn't that be great! That is the dream that many people hold somewhere deep inside of themselves as they deal with the day-to-day challenges. What we're looking for is relief from a survival mindset that keeps us locked in a constant struggle. If all your needs were satisfied, there is a strong possibility that your life would be more difficult and stressful than it is at present. The answer to get relief from overwhelm and stress is not making more money - that will create more stress. The answer you seek is inside you. A majority of the world population lives with a perception that life is difficult and complicated, and the entire struggle is anchored in our beliefs.

Our basic needs appear very simple: food, water, and shelter. We have other needs, (safety, love and belonging and esteem) and they complicate our lives and block us from our potential. My entire life was devoted to satisfying these additional needs without any awareness on my part. I was always doing what I needed to in order to get people's attention and approval because my idea of love was "being seen and accepted" by others. I was very good at achieving results and getting attention, but it never provided me with a sense of fulfillment, only a desire to get more attention. The driving force

43

inside me for the need to get attention was my desperate attempts to get an acknowledgment (which meant love) from my father. The competition was fierce in a family of six children. I am not sure that my siblings were competing with me, but that was my perception, and I did what I needed to do to get attention. At times I resorted to adverse actions that would always get the attention but it wasn't positive.

I was a very "needy" person for over 50 years, without any conscious awareness on my part. It was all part of my game of survival. When I got clarity about my "neediness," I was shocked to see how I was living life. It felt as if I was walking around with a "beggars cup" figuratively speaking, asking everyone to give me some love, let me belong, keep me safe and let me know you like me, please! I had been on my transformational path for over eight years at this time, and my new realization was crystal clear; I was very needy. When I saw how this was blocking me and the effect on my life I started making changes immediately. After fifty years of living in survival, neediness was very familiar to me. I came to learn very quickly that if I am needy, I eliminate the possibility of being responsible for myself. All of my decisions in life were influenced by my desire to get this "unknown" neediness satisfied. It was instinctively the primary factor behind every decision in my life without any conscious awareness on my part. I was trapped! No matter what actions I took or success I achieved, everything I did was to gain acknowledgment from others.

Our life is controlled by our needs when we live for anything that is "outside" of us. You are responsible from your skin in! Nothing "outside" of your skin is going to allow you to become more responsible; that is a choice we must make from our hearts. Nothing outside of us is going to deliver the self-fulfillment we seek. The path to self-actualization and living your true life purpose always starts in your heart. This is the most important paragraph in this book! Why? Because your needs and the stories that support your beliefs about needs are blocking you. You will come to learn why satisfying your physical needs is the source of your problem. When viewing your needs from a non-physical perspective, your entire life changes instantly. As you stop hoping that other people will make you feel better, you gain awareness on how to nurture yourself! Personal transformation requires one to start learning the process of being responsible for "everything" in your life, otherwise you will assume the role of a victim.

I was thrilled when I discovered Abraham Maslow's "Hierarchy of Needs." My transformation led me on a path that taught me how to transcend my life in the moment and not get trapped by focusing on my physical needs and desires. My experience has taught me how to access "true power," which is why I am writing this book. I have spent the last six years coaching others how to achieve this in their life, and my client's results have been nothing short of miraculous! When you are living your true life purpose the energy you share with the world is your authentic self-expression. When you familiarize yourself with all of the puzzle pieces required to achieve authentic self-expression, they snap together quickly, and your results improve instantly. There are only five pieces of the puzzle, and it creates a blueprint for you to follow that makes life simple.

"I teach powerful tools that allow you to create an authentic, responsible, and abundant life."

— *Bill Heinrich*

We learn to access a high level of spiritual consciousness; we are not learning how to achieve more success or make more money. Our spiritual consciousness is non-physical, and success and wealth are the trappings of a survival lifestyle in the physical world. To thrive, we must access our non-physical resources from our hearts and make choices that support our essence, our passion, our purpose and our prosperity. To achieve living at a higher vibration, we must "lighten our load" by discarding anything that is weighing us down and doesn't support a self-actualized life. I guarantee you that everything blocking you, holding you back and standing in your way are internal beliefs that support a survival mind-set and the perception of your needs.

I have desperately wanted to share this information for the past four years. I started writing this book four years ago but didn't publish it because it was too "Airy-Fairy"! I didn't have the teaching grounded and knew I was missing an important piece of information. What was missing was a physical component that would allow you to understand this information. Maslow's "Hierarchy of Needs" was the missing piece. The language I speak each day is foreign to anyone that is trapped focusing on their basic needs. Referencing Maslow's research of the five levels of basic needs is the foundation that will allow you to understand how to transform your life. Everything you need to live a self-actualized life is in this book and understanding what is blocking you is the most crucial aspect. Without awareness of your blocks and challenges, you can't make sustainable choices to transform and satisfy your sincere desire for self-fulfillment.

My personal experience and "proof of concept" research has revealed that we live in a society focused on survival. The perceptions of life we develop are based solely on surviving. Fulfilling our needs not only consumes our life, but it also controls and defines it. Your internal desire (survival) to fulfill your physical needs determines how you live your life. Maslow demonstrates that we must learn to satisfy our non-physical needs to achieve self-actualization. Gaining awareness of the characteristics of self-actualization activates another level of understanding, energy, and intention. Understanding each of the levels of human needs will allow you to make significant positive changes in your life and the first step in transforming your life is assessing your life at this time. The second step is to identify a new path to follow, and the third step is to start to build a new foundation that will support your new direction. Abraham Maslow's "Hierarchy of Needs." is a sound fundamental point of reference and this will be the foundation for our journey together exploring the "Seven Levels of Truth."

The "Hierarchy of Needs" is very accurate in describing how your struggles in life are created and how you can rise above your perceived problems and live with passion and purpose. The challenge is your current perception of how to fulfill your needs; it is essential to develop some guideposts that will light the path for you. I will share with you all of the tools that I use in my coaching business that achieve remarkable results with my clients. Once they understand the tools and resources I am going to share with you, their lives improve significantly, and it happens fast! I intend to share with you the best tools I use to accomplish this with every client. Your choices can yield the same results.

The key is simplicity, and as mentioned, the place to start is with Abraham Maslow's "Hierarchy of Needs" because we must establish common ground as our point of reference. I would like you to understand that it's not my intention to convince you that this is something everyone must do. Everyone is different! Take what you like and leave the rest. We've each have had different experiences in life so how you use this information to make lasting positive changes in your life is entirely up to you. I have been doing "proof of concept" research with these tools for the past six years. My focus has been to identify the most effective method to make sure this information can be understood, anchored and applied in your life on a daily basis.

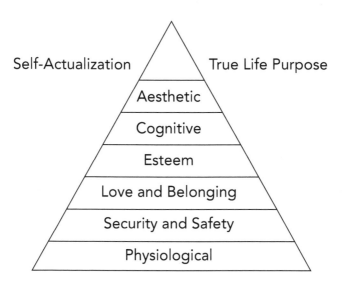

I love the simplicity of this pyramid. There are seven levels, and as you start at the bottom and go to the top, you will be familiar with the different levels of survival. At the top of the pyramid is self-actualization. Self-actualization is our need to achieve full expression of our innermost being. It's the path to our true life purpose. We each have very unique Divine Gifts, and our deepest desire is to discover our purpose and how to share it with the world, achieving the ultimate form of self-actualization! What Maslow's research revealed was that to achieve self-actualization we need to use a higher level of existence which he called self-transcendence.

Transcendence is a level of existence that allows you to rise above your current beliefs, perceptions, and understanding of survival or life as you know it. Transcendence will enable you to look objectively at what is currently blocking you in your life and learn to make choices that will lead directly to a self-actualized life. I am going to explain transcendence thoroughly in a later chapter in the book.

Why do you want to change? Are you trying to get away from discomfort and pain? Are you just curious? Maybe you are a seeker, already self-actualized and you want to live at a higher vibration. We are unique and have had experiences that are different. Even though we have experienced similar problems in our life, our perception of our experience is likely to be completely different. We each have different viewpoints on life, but we act as though everyone is the same. As you read this book, please keep in mind that how you use these tools is your choice and whatever you choose for you will be perfect for you. Our first step is to understand Abraham Maslow's "Hierarchy of Needs" thoroughly. In all of my research and "proof of concept" studies, one thing was consistent with everyone I assisted. We get stuck in survival! Regardless of your level of success, there are areas of your life where your survival beliefs are blocking you. We end up living a life of survival because this was the focus of our parents, family, caregivers and authority figures in our youth. Understanding the ingredients of the survival lifestyle is mandatory, so you know which changes and choices are going to have the most significant positive impact on your life.

For years I have been teaching the difference between surviving versus thriving. Surviving is living your life to fulfill your physical desires, and thriving is the use of non-physical resources to live a life of gratitude, peacefulness, abundance, and love. To move away from your perceptions of survival you are going to create a blueprint to follow that will lead you to self-fulfillment. Before you examine Maslow's "Hierarchy of Needs" I want to suggest that you research and study these further on your own. Maslow's work speaks for itself, and there is no need to examine it from a deeper psychological perspective, at this time. Maslow's basic list of needs is going to serve our purpose. However, taking time to research Maslow's work further may be beneficial to you, and any awareness you can gain will allow you to make new choices. I am going to give you tools and information that will put you firmly on the path to self-actualization and live your true life purpose.

As you review the "Hierarchy of Needs" examine each of the needs from a perspective of how critical that particular need is in your life and how attached you are to it! How do you prioritize these needs in your life on a daily basis? As you examine different aspects of your life as it pertains to your needs, you will see how the needs are intertwined, and they start to become more complicated when observed from a physical perspective.

Physiological

Our most basic needs are physiological. Air, water, food, shelter, sex, and excretion. When there is an absence of any of these most basic needs, there will be less satisfaction in life.

Safety

Our next level of needs is safety, and feeling safe in the present moment in in our physical surroundings. Maslow also references feeling safe with our financial, psychological, emotional, social and social aspects of our life including our careers. How many times have people told you "Drive safely" or "Have a safe flight." We use this word very loosely. Feeling safe is one of the most shocking topics that I discuss with my clients. They typically don't look at the different aspects of life as they relate to feeling safe. At the core of any disturbance in life is not feeling safe. It is necessary to create a secure foundation from which to change your life.

Belonging and Love

Belonging to a community creates a connection to relationships and love. It is from belonging to a community that we feel supported and can help others with compassion. Belonging to a community introduces us to the possibility of having a more intimate relationship with other people.

Esteem

As we achieve success, our confidence increases and we have a greater sense of self-worth, along with our need for recognition and acknowledgment.

Cognitive Needs

Acquiring knowledge, meaning, and understanding that will have a positive impact on your personal growth.

Aesthetic

Appreciation for the beauty, balance, and form in life that we choose to infuse into our lives.

Each of us has an internal desire for self-fulfillment. Maslow refers to self-actualization as a peak experience, reaching your potential and being happy with life. Notice that I've kept them each very simple, and there's a reason for that. This information is only to reference a standard foundation as we move forward towards transcendence. Because you will see how the needs become intertwined, misunderstood and create chaos, confusion, and fear in our lives.

Maslow's five levels of the "Hierarchy of Needs" prioritize our needs which will allow you to develop a blueprint that you can follow that will allow you to make more evolved and self-actualized choices in your life. Self-actualized individuals have characteristics that define how they choose to experience life. It is important to recognize that none of these characteristics refer to the physical results. (Process = 51 and Results = 49) They are all distinctly focused on the non-physical perception of our experience in life. They all speak to the "inner-game perception" without any focus on the actual physical result. These characteristics are all supportive of our greatest gift; free will, and choice.

> **"What a man can be, he must be, that we may call self-actualization."**
>
> — *Abraham Maslow*

Self-actualized people are typically making choices and expressing themselves from their heart. When you are speaking from your heart, you are connecting to your highest power and authentic self-expression. Our life purpose gets expressed with energy, and our heart creates the fuel that supports our intentions, purpose, and passion. When we speak directly of our expectations, we are addressing the physical results, which dis-empowers us. Speak in support of the energy that is fueling your intentions, not your goals or expectations. Our expectations are all about something we want like a car, more money, a vacation, beautiful clothes or a new place to live. When we speak from our heart, we are expressing who we are and that supports our intentions in life. Who you are is more meaningful, productive and fulfilling than what you have!

As I researched Maslow's work I found numerous articles about self-actualization. There were many different descriptions about how to live a self-actualized life. I chose two different articles that provide different perspectives on the characteristics of a self-actualized life. Becoming aware of these characteristics determines how effectively you are making choices as a self-actualized individual. Notice that none of the traits define physical expectations, or how the result will appear in physical form. The physical manifestations of our actions are secondary to the energy behind our efforts. Self-actualization is created through choice by understanding the logic that caused us to get stuck in survival. Living life from this perspective will allow you to transcend any situation in life to a better result. When we respond from a place of love we can create what appears to be miraculous results by remaining detached. Fear creates a desire to manipulate and control our conversations and actions so we can achieve our expectation or goal.

As you review these different characteristics of self-actualized individuals, notice your reaction to them and ask your heart to define the meaning of each one of these as it relates to your intentions in life.

Characteristics of Self-Actualization - Internet search Result #1[5]

- They are realistically oriented.

- They accept themselves, other people, and the natural world for what they are.

- They have a great deal of spontaneity.

- They are problem-centered rather than self-centered.

- They have an air of detachment and a need for privacy.

- They are autonomous and independent.

- Their appreciation of people and things is fresh rather than stereotyped.

- Most of them have had profound mystical or spiritual experiences, although not necessarily religious.

- Their values and attitudes are democratic.

- They do not confuse means with ends.

- Their sense of humor is philosophical rather than hostile.

- They have a great fund of creativeness.

- They resist conformity to the culture.

- They transcend the environment rather than just coping with it.

Source: Simple Psychology[5]

Characteristics of Self-Actualization - Internet search Result #2[6]

- Self-actualized people embrace the unknown and the ambiguous.

- They accept themselves, together with all their flaws.

- They prioritize and enjoy the journey, not just the destination.

- While they are inherently unconventional, they do not seek to shock or disturb.

- They are motivated by growth, not by the satisfaction of needs.

- Self-actualized people have a purpose.

- They are not troubled by the small things.

- Self-actualized people are grateful.

- Self-actualized people are humble.

- Self-actualized people resist enculturation.

- Despite all this, self-actualized people are not perfect.

Source: Huffington Post[6]

Can you see the difference between the perspective of surviving and thriving? Surviving focuses on what we will get, and thriving is focusing on how we can expand and enhance our life. Let's look at two examples from the list of characteristics:

Not confusing the means with the end.

Non-physical perspective: By remaining present and connecting with others as I move towards my intention I will make sure that my energy supports the best resolution/outcome for all involved.

Physical perspective: I am focused, and my focus is only on reaching my goal, and you can help me get what I want because I will be happier when I get it. Our favorite radio station is WIIFM! (What's In It For Me?).

Self-actualized people embrace the unknown.

Non-physical perspective: When I focus on generating positive energy into everything in my life, the results are always perfect. I can improve the outcome by focusing on the present moment with a loving, positive perception of finding the best outcome for all involved.

Physical perspective: What is happening? We must control the direction of our goal all the time, or we will not achieve the anticipate result. Manipulation and control are the cornerstone of survival!

When our perspective is attached to what the physical result will be, we are abandoning our power and working with force. If we stay detached and focus on each step with a positive, loving perception we know we can attract the perfect resources (physical and non-physical) to achieve results that will be much better than anything we could imagine. The power and influence of our energy are much more potent than an individual expectation. Learning to view life from a non-physical perspective is mandatory if you want to learn to transcend your life from surviving to thriving. Take a moment right now and go back and review the two lists of characteristics and compare each from a physical and non-physical basis. Notice how your energy changes when you find the perfect outcome for each trait when examined from a physical and non-physical perspective.

In the later years of his life, Abraham Maslow expanded the "Hierarchy of Needs" from five levels to seven levels. He realized that to access transcendence there are two more levels of needs that must be acknowledged, accessed and fulfilled. These two additional levels of needs are essential because they identify the characteristics required to transcend your life. We are going to an in-depth look at transcendence later in the book. The two additional levels that Maslow added to the "Hierarchy of Needs" are critical because there are requirements that must be fulfilled to use transcendence effectively. Our understanding of needs from a survival perception is going to block us, not allow us to transcend our lives. As you review the expanded "Hierarchy of Needs" I would like you to notice that each level of needs (except physiological needs) speaks only to a non-physical perception. Security needs speak to safety; social needs speak to love, affection and intimacy; esteem needs are recognition and achievement; cognitive needs are knowledge and meaning; aesthetic needs speak to beauty and balance.

Your mind (analytical) and your heart (feelings) will have different perceptions of these characteristics because your mind is giving you an opinion based on your past experiences in life, and your heart will respond in the present moment. As we move forward notice when you react cynically or immediately question something you have read. These quick reactions will show you areas that may need attention. You will have new perception of life after reading this book; referring back to your initial feelings will provide you with valuable information about how you experience life now. It's your understanding and utilization of these characteristics that will allow you to move up through the hierarchy of needs to self-actualization and transcendence. Self-actualization enables you to grow and transform your life as fast as you desire. Your choices determine the outcome.

"Your mind and your heart will each give you a different perspective of life. One is instinctive and the other is intuitive."

— Bill Heinrich

Make particular note of the top three characteristics developed through the research Abraham Maslow did towards the end of his life. The Hierarchy of Needs is expanded to seven levels to accommodate transcendence. There are additional characteristics required to achieve transcendence and Maslow has defined them very succinctly. As you move closer to transcendence, (soul-centered vs. ego-centered), you will be gaining an entirely new perspective on life. If we attempt to change how we perceive life from our survival based perception, we will only go around in circles! (Sound familiar?) Then we get stuck, blocked, frustrated and overwhelmed! The fastest way to change your life is to understand the difference between a physical and the non-physical perspective (we live in two different dimensions), keeping your perception focused on the non-physical to enhance your experience. Otherwise, you get locked into survival with your fundamental level of needs, and we are victims of life.

Developing a survival perspective makes you a victim, and you give away all of your power to someone else. Anytime you believe that someone caused you harm you are giving your power to that person. It is impossible to transcend your life when you're a victim. When you give your power away to someone else, you have lost control of your life. Becoming self-actualized the very first thing you do is take responsibility for your life, complete responsibility for everything in your life. Through your choices, you can change your life whenever you desire, but you must identify what you are replacing. With responsibility, you can create the life of your dreams, and as a victim, you help others build their dream life. I am 100% responsible for my life! Anyone and anything that is part of my life is because I chose it and I allow it. If there's someone or anything in my life creating chaos, problems, and disruptions, it is in my life because I am allowing it. Anything that is in your life you must own and be responsible for your choice that created it. This is a requirement to be self-actualized, and it is the path to individual freedom.

You will undoubtedly understand as you read this book that creating an understanding of the difference between the physical and non-physical aspects of your life will make your journey much more manageable and peaceful. As you make choices to transcend your life, you will be moving from the perspective that life is a linear physical experience to a view that includes the non-physical aspects of your life, which are the perceptions of your soul. The non-physical knows no boundaries and is only focused on energy and expansion. All of your power resides in the non-physical, and when you start accessing transcendence, you will see the effect of that power immediately. What's exciting is how fast this can happen. It is as simple as making a choice. Awareness and choice are the most powerful tools that support free will and allow you to be self-actualized and live your life purpose.

Earlier in this chapter I mentioned how excited I was when I found Maslow's "Hierarchy of Needs." For over five years I have been looking for a simple explanation that would be easy for others to understand so I can share these wonderful resources. All of the work that I've done for the past five years is from a non-physical perspective. In other words, I have been living life as a self-actualized individual that views life and makes choices from a non-physical perspective. During my transformation as I stopped being controlled by my lower level needs, I started opening myself to connect with the powerful resources of the universe. All of these resources are non-physical. With each choice I was continually surprised at how fast the results appeared. Using the non-physical resources I am sharing is exciting, and will impact you moment by moment, and with each choice you make. I assure you that you will believe in miracles after you understand transcendence and apply it in your life.

I discovered early in my transformation that I'm an energy empath. What does that mean? My perception of other people, places or things and events in my life are all influenced by the energy I feel as we interact. It's difficult to explain what happens inside me when I feel the external energy. I can feel whether the energy is fear or love, and if it's fear I'm able to identify the aspects of their life that are creating the fear. My empathic abilities started many years ago, but I didn't know what they were at first. Over time as I continue to gain awareness, I make choices that will increase my vibration and the level of sensitivity continues to grow. The choices I make in life come from an energetic perspective first and then the physical. As I learn to live with this energy and it continues to grow, I'm less attached to the physical world and more immersed in the non-physical world.

Now I realize that my access to higher wisdom caused me to be confused when I was a child because my perception of life comes from a source of wisdom which is based in the non-physical realm. As a child, this perception left me feeling that life didn't make sense to me. I thought there was something wrong with me because everyone was acting in a way (fitting in with society) that was foreign to me. Now I understand why but as a child in my family of origin I was lost. We have all come to earth to learn lessons, and this was my primary lesson. Once I decided to change my life I was continually guided to learn more and more about the most important part of life, the non-physical aspects.

When I came across the Abraham Maslow's work, I was very excited because it provided me with a safe portal into the physical world. It creates a model and a point of reference that will allow me to show you how to live an authentic, responsible and abundant life. Everything that I share with you about life will come from the "hierarchy of needs" perspective because we're living life in the physical, and that is where your point of reference is focused; physical survival! We are living life in the physical and we must stay in the physical and learn to flow self-actualized energy into our daily life. Many people that start to experience the non-physical through meditation, yoga and reiki have an attraction to "hang out" in the non-physical energy and cruise through life. We must remain in the physical world and allow that energy to flow into our physical life. Otherwise we become so spiritual that we are of no earthly use!

My energetic sensitivity allows me to identify energetic vibrations and determine whether or not having that vibration in my life is going to assist me with the expansion of my soul. It is impossible to be self-actualized when you're stuck in the basic level of needs. When someone comes in my life that is living in these lower levels of needs, it's in my soul's best interest not to have that energy in my life. We all have situations with family or at work where we feel stuck with these people. We feel obligated to allow them to remain in our life because of our upbringing. The truth of this matter is that you have the right to live your life in a way that you choose. When you have a blueprint, clarity, and direction, it becomes much easier to make choices that only support yourself energetically. When you have awareness, it is easy to transcend the energy and protect yourself from this energy when it is an integral part of your surroundings.

Here's an example; I found a dry cleaner near my home that was close, had reasonable prices and adequate turn-around time. The first time I used the dry cleaner when I went to pick my clothes up late one afternoon, there was no one at the counter. Then they had to search to find my clothes, and they were clean but not gathered together and covered. The next time I went back a different person was there, but I had a similar experience. It was undeniable that there was internal chaos based on the way they handled my transactions. My clothes were finished on time but not prepared (wrapped together) for me to pick them up. They were friendly people, and my clothes looked great! But, they scrambled around each time to gather the clothes and give them to me. It was chaotic, and I do not allow chaos in my life, and I certainly don't want chaos infused into my wardrobe! I didn't get upset and complain, I only observed if this was energy that supports the expansion of my soul. I found another dry cleaner that peacefully has my garments ready for me at the pre-determined time.

I would imagine some of you reading this book right now are thinking that the example I gave sounds extreme, weird or kind of crazy. And I can understand why you would be thinking that; you're thinking, and I'm feeling. The first ingredient and guidepost to a successful non-physical perception of life is the vibration/energy that we transmit. When I encounter a vibration that is draining me rather than energizing me, I can eliminate it. You will learn how the ego uses your head (mind) to control you with rationalizations. You will also learn that energy is just energy. It's just a vibration, and we can amp up that vibration by feeding it loving energy. If you have people, places or things in your life with negative energy, then that is who you are. Being self-actualized requires taking responsibility for your life and rising above survival in the physical, so your entire life isn't spent attempting to satisfy your material desires.

Surviving or thriving; which life do you choose to live? You have to choose one or the other, and if you can make a choice, you will select thriving. The people that are stuck in survival don't have the power of choice because they are accountable to (external) people, places and things that dictate what they do. Survival does not offer the luxury of choice, and it does not allow you to live consciously and take full responsibility for everything in your life. This isn't a judgment of your character, and it doesn't mean you're a terrible person. These are the characteristics of survival, and they all lead to a life of limitation with a focus on everything "outside" of you. Self-actualization is all about your "inner game." This book is showing you how to be every bit as powerful as you possibly can be while you are in physical form on earth. The vibration you generate in each moment of your life will allow you to expand and grow or shrink into a life of lack and limitation.

5) www.simplypsychology.com https://www.simplypsychology.org/maslow.html

6) www.huffingtonpost.com https://www.huffingtonpost.com/david-sze/maslow-the-12-characteris_b_7836836.html

Guideposts for Your Journey.

1. What areas of your life are you living in survival?

2. Which of the characteristics of self-actualization are you using today?

3. Which characteristics of self-actualization would improve your life? Choose three and write how you believe your life would be better if you held a loving non-physical perspective instead of your current perceptions.

CHAPTER THREE ~ Our Divine Gifts

This information is so powerful that it actually defies an explanation. Nothing I can say would adequately define the magic that happens in your life when you know how to identify, access and flow your Divine Gifts. Your Divine Gifts are the energy that creates your true life purpose. It is your spiritual DNA! This is the energy that will allow you to be aligned with your highest power while in physical form (life). This is the missing puzzle piece for your life! I have never worked with a client that knew about their Divine Gifts prior to working with me. The moment they learned about their Divine Gifts the puzzle piece started snapping together. We got distracted by learning how to live in survival because our Divine Gifts are the exact opposite of a life of survival. When you flow your Divine Gifts, the only outcome can be abundance! Your seven Divine Gifts combine to create an energy that flows to you and through you with every breathe you take. If you were a radio station, your Divine Gift energy would be the signal you send out to attract listeners. When you are living in survival you block the signal (your energy) by maintaining your focus on the material world, and living in survival.

Thriving is your birth-right! It is who you are; it is your essence. Every aspect of surviving in life is in direct conflict with your being. You are spiritual beings having a human experience. You don't have a soul, you are a soul, and you have a body. This is why understanding the non-physical aspect of your life is so important. Your life purpose is an energy that flows through you and when you connect to this energy your life changes instantly! I am sharing all of the ingredients you need to use in your life, and you get to determine how much of each ingredient to use. When identifying an internal belief that causes you to choose survival and you make a different choice that moves you toward thriving, you are allowing more of your Divine Gift energy to flow and you increase your power. Living life in survival is like riding in a "little red wagon" and thriving using your Divine Gifts is like riding in a Lamborghini! Fasten your seat belt! This isn't the answer to life's biggest question but is the "secret sauce" that makes the answer so powerful. The first step is becoming aware of all of the resources that I am sharing in this book.

You are powerful beyond measure! Connecting with the power of your Divine Gifts requires that you learn how to integrate this powerful energy into your current life. It requires letting go of some old familiar patterns of behavior that supported survival. It's not as difficult as you may think because connecting to your Divine Gifts is priceless. There are seven Divine Gifts and I refer to them as the Seven Levels of Truth. Each of these Divine Gifts has its own level of energy and specific purpose. These are the gifts that you are here to share with the world. You don't have to search for your Divine Gifts; they are flowing through you right now! As you are consumed by survival, you are lead away from your Divinity, and leading you with no direct knowledge of this resource. This energy isn't external energy that you encounter occasionally; it's an internal energy that makes up your "Breathe of Life." It is your energetic blueprint.

"Our deepest fear is not that we are inadequate. Our deepest fear is that we are powerful beyond measure. It is our light, not our darkness that most frightens us."

— *Marianne Williamson*

We possess powers that are beyond our wildest imagination and a limited belief in what we are truly capable of accomplishing. Our attachment to the physical keeps us in a state of limitation, and our ego creates fear to hold us back. When we detach from the physical and focus our energy on our intentions and being of service to others, the magic will start to happen. Most people believe that their life purpose is what they "do" for a career in their life. The reason we create this belief is that we have been conditioned to stay focused on the physical side of life and there is so much attachment to how others view our career, and we label it as our purpose. Our life purpose is not what we are "doing" rather it is the energy behind our thoughts, words, and actions. We are human beings, not human doings! When we are flowing the energy of our divine gifts into our career in daily activities; we will be living our true life purpose.

This may seem difficult to understand, but once you have this experience, you will realize why it's difficult to describe.

We each have seven Divine Gifts; we all have the same gifts. We have the same seven Divine Gifts, but we each have different proportions of each Divine Gift. No two people are the same! We each have our own specific spiritual DNA, the unique combination of our seven Divine Gifts. Have you ever heard that you have a unique gift to share with the world? That gift is the outward expression of your spiritual DNA (Divine Gifts) into the world in service to others.

I will go into detail about the seven Divine Gifts in a moment but first, let me tell you how I learned about the Divine Gifts. I attended a seminar offered by a friend, Andrrea Hess in Scottsdale, Az., about six years ago. The workshop was about manifesting abundance by connecting to our soul energy. At the beginning of the seminar, Andrrea gave us our Divine Gifts, and from the moment I started to read about the Divine Gifts, it ignited a memory which might be from a past life experience. It opened a world of knowledge that I have about the Divine Gifts. The day before I had no conscious awareness of the Divine Gifts and the next day I could teach a class on the Divine Gifts! Every time I thought about the divine gifts, more knowledge appeared. I have been researching, studying and exploring the Divine Gifts daily since that day.

The only plausible explanation for the immediate depth of knowledge that appeared is that I worked with the Divine Gifts in a past life. It was the same as waking up one morning and realizing that you are now fluent in a foreign language, without explanation. My depth and breadth of knowledge were shocking to me. I knew immediately what the Divine Gifts were, how they worked and the impact they can have in our lives. I was captivated by how easy it is to connect to our authentic power using our Divine Gifts. I immediately realized that I must learn how to share this power with others. But I didn't know how to teach others in a manner that would allow them to hold on to this magical energy and be able to access it at will. I shared with different people in the beginning, and I went through their gifts with them, and everyone had a fantastic experience, but they couldn't maintain that state of being. When I spoke to them three or four weeks later, they had lost the "mojo." The experience was great, but it had no lasting effect.

I immediately realized that I had to develop a blueprint that would allow people to integrate these gifts permanently into their lives. I realize that we can't live in our Divine Purpose 100% of the time. It isn't possible. We are living on earth and our lives are filled with interruptions and disruptions. But it was disappointing to see someone a few weeks later after doing an empowerment consultation with them, and they had lost contact with the energy. I needed to figure out a manner to deliver this information so it would stick. I have successfully developed the blueprint that works after many years of "proof of concept" testing.

To access your Divine Gifts, you must understand the universal laws and become more knowledgeable about the non-physical side of life. To utilize your divine gifts, you must follow the operating guidelines of the universe. The objective is to learn to access all of the resources that the universe has to offer. We live in two different dimensions; one is physical, and the other is non-physical. The physical dimension is life on earth. The non-physical dimension is acknowledging universal energy. There are many examples of non-physical energy. And like cellular telephones, we each have our own signal (vibration), and our signal is assigned a number. I don't analyze the technical and engineering aspects of a cell phone when I dial a number. I use it as it is intended and marvel at the how technology has expanded! I can be connected "non-physically" to someone on the other side of the world, with a phone call or video call, in seconds! There is more happening in the "non-physical" dimension than in our physical reality.

Since the day I learned about the Divine Gifts it has been my intention to write this book. Not for fame or fortune, but to share with you the most powerful experience you can have in life. My objective is to "empower" other people in the same manner that I have been "empowered." This will spread quickly as soon as it gets recognized. Imagine what the world will be like with more people living their true life purpose! I have seen the difference with my client's lives. As they go through a "life purpose" change, they influence hundreds of people in their circles of connections.

It took a long time to identify all of the elements necessary to accomplish my objective. Through my research and "proof of concept" I have developed a blueprint that allows you to access these resources forever. What's fascinating to me is that people immediately understand "the energy" when I explain it to them. Not only has it been with you your entire life, but the energy is also you! This is who you are - an energetic being that is here to share your unique gifts with the world, your Divine Gifts. Someone immersed in survival will have great difficulty understanding the Divine Gifts. This is something that must be experienced and once experienced it is never forgotten. This Divine Energy is so powerful and magical that I give all of my clients a 100% guaranteed success rate and I let the client define the guarantee! If you commit to using the tools and information I am sharing, and apply them in your life, you'll live a life beyond your wildest dreams. This is not an exercise to get you excited and all "pumped up"! This is the "real deal," and every claim I am making is true. Everyone that I have worked with had the same opinion about this information, and they all say "it is priceless."

"We each have the same seven Divine Gifts, but in different proportions."

— *Bill Heinrich*

You don't need to learn how to use your Divine Gifts. That's the irony! You know how to use your Divine Gifts because the energy is you! What you must learn are the elements that have diverted you away from your Divinity. You must understand what is blocking the energy and you not allowing it to flow through you. This is the secret to living your life purpose; learn what is preventing you from accessing your power. This is where the adventure in life begins because everyone gets to use the recipe differently, in a manner that works for them. We each get to move at our own pace and pursue our life purpose as we choose.

The Seven Divine Gifts

Divine Compassion

Taking actions that support our fundamental needs.

Divine Creation

Your daily actions demonstrate how to bring thought into physical form.

Divine Order

Mixing style and grace with structure and process. You bring balance, harmony, order, and peace to yourself and others.

Divine Healing

Bringing energy to light that we are perfect, we are not damaged and never have been.

Divine Authentic Self Expression

Creating new perceptions for others using the written and spoken word.

Divine Truth

You have a gift of seeing situations as they truly are.

Divine Power

The ability to manifest unlimited abundance through free will and choice.

As you experience this information, notice how you feel. Simply accept the Divine Gifts and the concept of this energy flowing through you. Your Divine Gifts are the energetic essence of who you are. You don't need to learn how to use the Divine Gifts because it is only necessary to create an awareness of them. Your divine gifts is an integral part of your life force. Different cultures describe life force with different words. The Chinese call it "Chi," The Hawaiians refer to our life force as "Ha" and India refers to it as "Prana." From a non-physical spiritual perspective, your purest form of life force is flowing the energy of your Divine Gifts in their proper proportion which is Divine Energy in physical form.

When you look at your Divine Gifts from the physical, you start to think (thinking is where we go wrong) about how to practice using these Divine Gifts to improve your life. Don't do that! You don't need to practice using the energy of these Divine Gifts; just let it flow; you breathe this energy! You only need to identify what is blocking you from this energy. The Divine Gifts can only be accessed, described and expressed from a non-physical perspective. Understanding the difference between a physical and non-physical perspective is your objective. This is why I was so excited when I saw Abraham Maslow's "Hierarchy of Needs." Maslow explains how to achieve self-actualization, and the most potent form of self-actualization is living in your Divinity, that is the highest vibration available to you.

We came to earth with these Divine Gifts, and it is time we each acknowledge and express our unique Divinity. When we are using our Divine

Gifts as intended, allowing these energies to flow through us into the physical, we become ageless and timeless. This is known as Authentic Self-Expression, infusing our thoughts, words, and actions with Divine energy. We are here to be of service to others while remaining present, knowing the results will be for the benefit of all. This is how we create abundance in our lives because when you are flowing your Divine Energy, the only outcome can be abundance. Authentic self-expression is our Divine Truth. When people refer to speaking their truth, they are typically just giving us their opinion, because their perspective is in the physical and our focus will be on our expectations which are outside of us. Our authentic self-expression is just a flow of energy with no attachment to the results. There's a world of difference between these two experiences. When we're flowing our Divine energy, we are living life in the highest form possible.

As this energy flows to us now, it is not recognized because we are examining it from our physical perspective and we don't realize that it's our most powerful resource on earth. When the energy flows to us and gets blocked from its intended purpose, the physical results will appear as negative. I refer to this as dysfunctional Divine Energy which is an oxymoron because there's nothing about the Divine that's dysfunctional. This is how you can start to identify which gifts are yours because you will be familiar with the negative aspects you have experienced in the past. Each of the seven Divine Gifts has negative characteristics that are an indication the energy is being blocked and not recognized.

Behavior Associated with Blocking the Seven Divine Gifts

Divine Compassion:

Incapable of saying no when asked to help.

Over identified with those you serve, lose your identity.

Divine Creation

Lost in thoughts and fears, bogged down and stuck.

Mis-alignment to your purpose impact finances negatively.

Divine Order

You hate it when people are upset with you.

You will do whatever is necessary to avoid drama.

Divine Healing

Take on the role of the martyr and quietly becoming resentful.

Start seeing the world as takers.

Divine Authentic Self-Expression

Feeling ignored, you give the same advice again and again and again.

If not constructive your advice will be inappropriate.

Divine Truth

People don't seem to have an interest in what you say.

You tend to become more aggressive and outspoken.

Divine Power

You get caught in the bright shiny object syndrome.

There are so many choices, and you don't want to eliminate any.

One of the reasons I did so much proof of concept work and delayed publishing this book was my desire to make certain you could understand and apply these resources in your life. I intend to empower you, not to confuse you. Keep in mind as you read about this information that the key to your success is working with your feelings and emotions (energy in motion). Your head can only access past experiences and the logic or story associated with the experience, which keeps you in survival. The energy created by your Divine Gifts is infinite potential, power, and love that immediately has access to all that is. You need only focus on flowing this energy; it is that simple. Flow your Divine energy and expect miracles.

We each have all seven of Divine Gifts, but we have them in different proportions. Experiences have shown me that we typically have three primary Divine Gifts that make up the majority of our divinity. Our largest gift is about 40%, our second by size is about 25%, and the third gift is about 15%. The remaining four Divine Gifts make up the remaining percentage in various proportions. All of the energies of our Divine Gifts are integrated together. It's like following a recipe to make a cake; we have different ratios of multiple ingredients. We mix the ingredients as instructed and end up with the finished product. If we use too much of one of the ingredients or not enough of one of the other ones, the outcome will not be as intended.

When we flow the energy of our gifts we must flow them in their proper proportion or our results will not be pleasant. It is quite common for us to over-identify with just one of the gifts because Divine Energy is an integral part of us and it feels so good when we get connected to it, even if it is just one aspect or portion. As I work with clients, I always review the dysfunctional side of their Divine Gifts first. Why? With the energy blocked you can only experience the adverse effects.

My advice to you is to identify with the negative aspects of your Divine Gifts each day; and this will show you what energy you are blocking and create a clear path to your life purpose.

As you refer to the dysfunctional aspects of Divine energy keep in mind that the negative behaviors become much more complicated than the examples given. The easiest way to identify these in your life is to keep this process simple. Only one of two negative behaviors can be occurring in your life: you're doing the exact opposite, or you've become completely absorbed by the Divine Gift. Don't get caught up in the little negative details, instead look at the big picture and then observe your behaviors to see how they are supporting this overall negative theme. The same is true for using your Divine Gifts; make a choice and see if your favorite is supporting your Divinity or if it is taking you away from your true life purpose.

Let's look at the Divine Gifts (Seven Levels of Truth) in more detail.

Divine Compassion

Positive: This energy is intended to help others with their most basic needs. It is about family, society, plants, and animals. The energy is very communal, and your compassionate empathy created by this energy is incredibly compelling to others.

Negative: You have a tendency to take on other people's issues and get lost in trying to help them. People with compassion as one of their more substantial gifts typically are unable to say "NO" when it appears assistance is needed. You find your love by helping others, but when doing this, you abandon yourself entirely. If you're not helping somebody else, you will probably feel lost.

Divine Creation

Positive: This is an energy that teaches others about the value of our experience on the journey, in the present moment. Everything comes from nothing, and Divine Creation is the energy that fuels our manifestations and teaches us the process of how to bring thought into physical form. When you have this energy, you will love any new experiences in the physical world. The physical world, not the digital world, will bring more success, it's all about how to create in the physical.

Negative: People with this energy typically have massive amounts of information streaming through their head all the time. This creates stress because you feel as though you should be acting on the ideas but there are too many, and it causes you to feel inadequate and overwhelmed.

Over a time the intensity of your emotional life could cause you to wallow in your emotions rather than releasing them constructively. When this happens it is likely you would get overwhelmed by life and get 'frozen" and take no action. Being misaligned with this energy creates adverse financial consequences.

Divine Order

Positive: This is an energy that creates harmony and balance in every area of your life. You like to do everything in an organized and structured manner. You help others realize the beauty of form and functionality and not only do things have to function harmoniously, they have to look beautiful also.

Negative: Anything that does not create harmony, balance, beauty, and love is upsetting to you! If there is a conflict with anyone, at any time you will avoid the conflicting energy like the plague. Drama upsets order, harmony, and balance that you breathe into life. This energy could cause you to become obsessive trying to do everything perfectly.

Divine Healing

Positive: This is an energy that makes you an expert at being in relationship with others. You make others feel whole and not broken, and you love being with people because people trust you and you are non-judgmental. You radiate this healing energy; it's just who you are.

Negative: You will over-give, become depleted and then get resentful at the people you have been serving. When you give, you are secretly hoping that others give back in return and at the same time you are not open to receive. You could take on the role of the martyr.

Divine Authentic Self-Expression

Positive: This is an energy of a spiritual teacher using the written or spoken word. Your authentic self-expression means you would be a great marketing person, salesperson or teacher. It's an energy of giving people "Aha" moments due to your unique ability to communicate in a manner that others understand. Originality is vital to you. Authentic self-expression requires the language of the heart.

Negative: You will tend to speak up, just to be heard even if what you're saying is inappropriate. You will also hide out as a student because you're afraid to start teaching. You will have a negative attitude because you don't feel heard by others.

Divine Truth

Positive: This is an energy of one who takes a stand for each person's truth. Your innate intention is to help understand and live their Divine Truth.

Negative: You could tend to be very "black and white in your opinions and express them in an abrasive manner. Or, you may respond by sitting silently knowing that if you started to speak, you would be more aggressive or outspoken than is appropriate at that time.

Divine Power

Positive: This is an energy that shows other people how powerful we are using our free will and choice. You probably have an instinctive sense of energy. You are excellent at manifesting because you know it's as simple as making a choice. You're probably very intuitive; you might even be psychic.

Negative: You suffer from the bright shiny object syndrome. There are just too many choices to decide because you don't want to lose out by making the wrong choice. You would tend to stay busy doing different things but it ends up being the same old thing, and nothing gets accomplished. You could also manage to take on too many responsibilities because you have a desperate need to be productive.

My research and "proof of concept" experience has shown me that we have predominant Divine Gifts that make up about 80% of our Divinity and the other four Divine Gifts are smaller. This is important because the more substantial the proportion of the Divine Gift, the more significant the dysfunctional behavior will be in your life.

Your Divine DNA defines all of the seven Divine Gifts and the varying degree or amount of each Divine Gift you possess. We each have a distinctly different Divine DNA; no two are the same. All are equal, and no gift or Divine DNA is better than the next. What matters is how you express them; actions speak louder than words. When you are expressing your Divine Gifts life seems timeless and ageless, and you are consumed by your ability to assist others doing what you love. But it is difficult to stay in this Divine space because of all of the distractions and challenges that are typical in life.

"Your life purpose isn't about who you are, your life purpose is an expression of how you are!"

— Bill Heinrich

When your energies and actions are expressed through your Divine Gifts into the physical, it can only result in abundance. Abundance is always the outcome of taking action that supports your Divinity. The purest form of authentic self-expression is displayed in your life as you are living your Divine Purpose. The energy is beautiful and magnetic to others. People notice that something is different, and they are not sure what it is, but they love how they feel. Divine Energy is powerful, and your soul's purpose is to express your Divine Gifts authentically into this lifetime.

I work with people who are "spiritual healers" and they always "think" that Divine Healing is their primary gift. I have never found that to be true! This is how we get detoured by the ego and our physical perceptions. We each have seven Divine Gifts, and we use them in service to others. It's the utilization of all seven Divine Gifts that allows healing to occur; we are the conduit, our commitment is to deliver this energy into the world. The physical outcome is not ours to determine, so we remain detached and share our Divine Gifts with the world.

Case Study of The Divine Gifts Integrated

Even people who are living a committed spiritual life can be deceived by the ego. They think their life purpose and unique gift is what they see as the result of their actions. Let me give an example: I did a Divine Purpose coaching session for someone who is exceptionally accomplished and known worldwide in the area of healing. They were certain that their Divine Gift was Divine Healing, but they were mistaken! This is a person that has won numerous awards and has been doing this work for many years. The truth for this person is that their actual gifts are Authentic Self-Expression, Power, and Creation and the result of their expression of these gifts has healed thousands of people. Even though their work appears in the physical world as "healing" and it does heal people, their gift is not Divine Healing. The physical perspective likes to judge our results, (our ego wants to celebrate). Their Divine Gifts are Divine Self-Expression, Divine Power and Divine Creation (listed in order of size). They were flowing their power through their authentic self-expression. There is no question they have a small amount of healing as a Divine Gift, but it is overwhelmed by the other more substantial gifts. Our ego wants to define everything, that is how it controls (protects) us! When we express our Divine Gifts as they are intended, it will be without concern for results. We only need to communicate them with love, and the results will many times appear miraculous.

Remember this is energy we are flowing, and our point of reference is our heart and our feelings. Your emotions are the compass you will use to navigate the physical world and stay connected to the non-physical world simultaneously. Stay in touch with how you feel and allow loving energy to fuel your thoughts, words, and actions. Our only job is to connect with as much of this Divine energy as possible and as often as we can. Integrating the Divine Gifts into your life is a powerful experience and it's fun to experiment with this loving energy.

Not only do our Divine Gifts bring us joy and happiness, they come with more exciting secrets and mysteries that unfold as time passes. First, we need to know how to identify our Divine Gifts and then how to integrate our Divine Gifts in our daily lives. When the student is ready, the teacher appears. We are going to examine (in a later chapter) how our life lessons block us from our Divine Gifts, and we each have life lessons to learn. We came to earth with these Divine Gifts, and it is time we each acknowledge our unique gift and share it with the world. This is who we are;

Divine Beings having a human experience.

Have you ever behaved in a manner that was surprising to you and then wondered why you acted like that? This happens as a result of a build-up of unexpressed Divine Energy that needs to be expressed and releases through negative behavior. Earlier I referred to the dysfunctional side of our Divine Gifts. Our Divine Gifts are not dysfunctional! The energy gets contaminated when it reaches us because we have it blocked. It is dysfunctional only in the way we release it into the world unconsciously. Another issue I have witnessed many times is people getting connected to the energy of just one of their Divine Gifts. Your life will be entirely out of balance when you are connected to just only one gift because the other energies are not accessed. It is the dysfunctional expression of your Divine Gifts (behavior that does not support you) that will allow you to get a glimpse of your Divinity. If you aren't living your Divinity, you are getting dysfunctional results because this Divine Energy is always flowing into your life.

Dysfunctional Individual Divine Gifts Case Study

This is worth another quick review because there are many different ways that dysfunctions show up when you aren't connected to your Divine Gifts. Here is a list of short case studies and the challenges my clients were experiencing. Remember that Divine Energy is not dysfunctional! When the energy flows through you and you are not aware of it, you contaminate the energy and it becomes dysfunctional.

When you examine the Divine Gifts imagine that you are measuring

your results on a scale from one to ten. One is total dysfunction (no

connection to your Divinity), and ten is living your Divinity.

DIVINE GIFT	EXTREME DYSFUNCTION	HIGHEST DIVINE ENERGY
Compassion	You can't say no! You get your love by taking care of other people.	This energy is grounded in helping others (people, animals, the earth) with their most basic needs with healthy boundaries.
Creation	Locked down in your emotions and unable to move forward. Or, you are creating obsessively.	Always focused on "the experience" of creating, knowing that each step creates more clarity and potential.
Order	You are very disorganized and chaotic or you run away from conflict and need to make everyone happy.	Your presence radiates harmony, balance, order and peace.
Healing	The world is full of "Takers," you are bitter and disappointed.	Your presence radiates loving acceptance and non-judgemental empathy.
Authentic Self Expression	Feeling ignored you give the same advice again and again.	A spiritual Teacher who uses written and spoken words to teach.

DIVINE GIFT	EXTREME DYSFUNCTION	HIGHEST DIVINE ENERGY
Truth	Judgmental, Outspoken and Aggressive - Not feeling heard	Humbly supportive of each person's unique truth.
Power	Can't Make a Decision, to many options & Possibilities	You manifest quickly and create your powerful life experience through free will & choice.

Divine Compassion - Mary didn't want to live, there was nothing to live for because her entire life was wrapped around helping others. Mary was unable to say no to a request to help. In fact it got much worse because when ever she "saw" anyone that needed assistance she automatically reacted, even without a request from the other person. Mary did not even exist! She had no life of her own! Her entire life was focused on getting love from others by taking care of everyone!

Divine Creation - John has a never-ending flow of creative energy that is always providing him with new ideas! He remains frustrated due to his inability to follow through on his ideas and the continuous flow of new information. He eventually become emotionally overwhelmed, depressed and stopped taking action all together. Or, John would start to take actions and create obsessively.

Divine Order - I worked with Elizabeth, an artist who had an innate understanding of beauty, balance, function and harmony. She was told as a child and an adult that being an artist was foolish, it was no way to create a proper life. Her internal anger toward the people who crushed her true life purpose, caused her to only create chaos in her life. Another client, Peter was so deeply connected to Divine Order that he literally ran away from confrontations and drama because it was so upsetting to his orderly energy, drama terrified him!

Divine Healing - Thomas was completely "wrapped up" in serving others but was resentful because he felt he didn't receive proper acknowledgement from those he served. He viewed himself as a martyr and secretly resented his clients and he would never open up to receiving because he was disillusioned. As he worked with other people he was actually "taking" from them because he was more interested in his well-being and getting acknowledged.

Divine Authentic Self-Expression - David is a brilliant spiritual teacher but was afraid to expose himself, his beliefs and wisdom because he didn't believe he had much to offer. As a result he remained in his "Spiritual Kingdom" journaling, channeling and never sharing his wisdom. People who have a larger proportion of this Divine energy have a tendency to hide out in seminars and then they can avoid teaching seminars themselves..

Divine Truth - Jerry's primary Divine Gift was Divine Truth and he was always judging everyone else. His opinions when spoken were typically direct and to the point, delivered harshly. He was constantly bothered by other people's ignorance.

Divine Power - Brian was buried in financial fear, created by beliefs of other family members. He was afraid to make a choice and commit to a plan of action for fear of criticism. He was stuck at an income level he couldn't break through and his life was being consumed negatively by the energy of survival. He stayed real busy but there was no real productivity, just a different look to the same old thing.

These are some actual case studies from clients (the names have been changed) I have worked with in the past. They give you a basic insight to some of their challenges. There is much more to add to each of theses stories. Our Divine Gifts are one part of the solution, the other pieces required are addressed in the remaining chapters of this book.

When you focus on flowing this energy into everything you think, say, and do, your life improves instantly. There is no limit to the amount of peace, love, joy and freedom that you can experience while flowing your Divine Gifts. There's an infinite amount of energy available, and your purpose is to flow as much of this energy as possible in your daily lives. As you learn to remove the blocks, you create a wider passage for energy to flow and to connect with your Divine Gifts. When you are expressing your Divine Gifts, you will be consumed by gratitude for the powerful way that you serve others. When you are using your Divine Gifts in service to others, you automatically experience an inner bliss and knowing that only comes from connecting to these energies. This is such a beautiful experience, and it is very humbling.

Be patient. Your view of the world today is going to change over time. When you are using your feelings as the first indication of the flow of energy, you will rapidly gain new perceptions. It is difficult to stay in this Divine space at first because you are accustomed to living in survival. You will become acutely aware of all of the distractions and challenges that you encounter every day. Some are generated by people around you, but most are a result of your inner beliefs and stories. These distractions and problems are essential for your personal growth; they immediately show which direction to follow that supports your Divinity. I will discuss life's disruptions in another chapter.

You know how to express your Divinity; it is the essence of who you are! You don't need operating instructions. It's far more important to become aware of what's blocking you. As you learn more about what's blocking your energy you can make choices that allow more of your Divine energy to flow. There are guideposts that you can follow on your journey that give you a reasonable assessment of your energy, your purpose, and intentions. The guidepost that I like and which seems the simplest to me is determining if I am looking at life from a physical perspective (what's in it for me), rather than viewing life from a non-physical perspective, (wanting to know how I can serve you). These two perspectives are opposites of each other.

It is essential to stay on earth and serve others. Don't use this energy to expand your spiritual experience into other dimensions for your enjoyment. You are experiencing life. You are on earth. You are here to serve others with a unique gift. This can only happen if you remain focused on your non-physical life and flow your Divine Gifts into your life in physical form.

We came to earth to learn lessons, and we each have our life lessons to learn. Once we understand the nature and scope of our life lessons, we can use our Divine Gifts to get past our lessons very quickly, if we choose to. The next chapter is focused on our life lessons.

Guideposts for Your Journey.

1. Do you identify with any of the negative and dysfunctional behaviors? Find the three Divine Gifts/dysfunctional behaviors that you are most familiar with?

2. Do you have the belief that your life purpose is the work you do? How would your life change if you intended to flow your Divine Energy and allow your life purpose to be expressed by your Authentic Self-Expression?

3. Have you ever practiced detachment, and only focused on the energy that fuels your thoughts, words, and actions, knowing your results will be perfect? How do you do this now? What can you do to be more present and support yourself with your divinity?

CHAPTER FOUR ~ Our Life Lessons

When I reflect on my life, the one thing that had the most significant positive impact on my life was learning that we each have a life lesson. I never understood life! It did not make sense to me. I now know why it didn't make sense to me and quite frankly I thought there was something wrong with me, like I was crazy! The fact that life didn't make sense to me was not an open topic for discussion; I kept that to myself. I found ways to survive while this belief remained hidden deep inside me. I didn't believe I could explain myself to anyone and have them understand me. I was only focused on surviving in an environment where I did not fit in. It all seemed so foreign to me. I finally reached the point, after decades of misery, that I had to find out why I was so miserable. That's when my transformation journey began and when I made a choice to find answers; I went all in. I spent the vast majority of my time focused solely on my transformation, and nothing else mattered.

About nine months after I began my spiritual journey someone introduced me to a book that changed my life. The book is called "The Life You Were Born to Live" written by Dan Millman. The book described the exact life I was living and all of the struggles I faced. I was thrilled that there was nothing wrong with me and I wasn't crazy. My life changed at that moment. Right in front of me was a book that described my life quite precisely, identifying my challenges and misery. How can this be? It was as if Dan Millman was looking over my shoulder following me around and making notes of all the struggles, frustrations and fears I had experienced.

The resources I am sharing with you are all powerful and must be integrated into your life, but the essential support is "The Life You Were Born to Live." All of our challenges, problems, discontentment and struggles are happening in our lives continuously. Why? Because we are alive and living on earth and we have come here to learn lessons. Our focus must remain on the physical portion of life, flowing our energy into our lives in every moment possible. Our challenges and problems are not going to go away! Life is about overcoming challenges and how we handle each challenge will determine the level of peacefulness in our life.

The problems don't go away, but our perceptions of the issues and challenges are going to change rapidly. Accessing our Divine Gifts allows us to overcome any obstacles and find a solution that is best for all involved. That is accomplished with any situation in life. Knowing our life lessons allows us to remain focused on specific areas that we know create our challenges. The key to personal change and transformation is awareness. Understanding what is causing a problem allows us to make different choices. When we are applying the characteristics of a self-actualization in our lives, we have the tools to make this adjustment to our life and eventually to our perceptions.

Do you believe in reincarnation? It is the belief that we continue to come back to earth to heal our soul through the lessons we learn on earth until we have learned all of our lessons and healed our soul. I don't know if reincarnation is true, but I do know we have life lessons. It is very obvious to me now that we are living life with specific lessons to learn. My focus now is the positive aspects of my life lessons as described in "The Life You Were Born To Live." My only interest is learning more about my current life experience and identifying resources that allow me to create peace, joy, freedom, and abundance in my life today. The path that is going to bring me more happiness is through my life lessons. Until I understand these lessons very thoroughly, I am not capable of making choices that lead to a peaceful and abundant life. With awareness of my lessons and the ability to flow my Divine Gifts, I can step across my lessons as they appear because I know the blueprint to follow. When I choose to step through a life lesson, the power of the lesson is diminished, and the energy of my Divinity is expanded. At the same time the challenge melts away and gets resolved simply, lovingly and peacefully. We each have specific life lessons to learn. This I know to be true.

There is no better time than right now to practice open-mindedness while we examine a possible path for the journey of our soul. I am aware that the topic of reincarnation when discussed publicly, gets immediate reactions, mostly against this theory, while a belief in reincarnation is held strongly by others. There doesn't seem to be any middle ground on this topic. My interest is in creating a blueprint for life that people can use to avoid the pitfalls, realize self-fulfillment and live self-actualized life. It doesn't matter if reincarnation is real, rather what matters is understanding what is blocking you from living the most powerful life possible today. Stay open-minded as we review life lessons; it takes us to an exciting discovery.

"Until we recognize and live in accord with our underlying purpose, our life may feel like a puzzle with missing pieces."

— Dan Millman, "The Life You Were Born to Live"

"The Life You Were Born to Live" is about numerology and describes the 37 different paths of life. Our life path can be identified using our date of birth! I was utterly captivated by this book because it allowed me to understand my challenges and make better choices in my life, immediately. For the first time in my life, I had some understanding of my life. It also led me to understand that everything in the universe is connected and there is a much higher plan. I began researching numerology in earnest. There are many different types of numerology; some use the date of birth and others use your legal name at birth, and they arrive at similar results regarding a persons' life path. I found that "The Life You Were Born to Live" was quite simple to understand and didn't delve into a complex spiritual hypothesis. Simple is better when we are searching for direction in life.

How does numerology work? Write out your birth date in individual numbers. If your date of birth is April 18, 1980 (04.18.1980) now add the single numbers (0+4+1+8+1+9+8+0= 31). Numerology only works with the single digit numbers of "1" - "9" and each of the individual numbers represent different life lessons. Now you add the two numbers in your total together (3+1=4). My numerology or my birth date stated in a numerological manner is 27/9. Twenty-seven is my birthdate numbers listed individually and added up, they equal 27, and the "9" is the sum of my other two birth numbers, 27 (2+7= 9). The two represents cooperation and balance, the seven represents Trust and Openness, and nine is my overall life lesson which represents Integrity and Wisdom.

When I look at my life expressed this way, through cooperative actions, I will learn to trust myself and be an open book in the way I share myself. These two lessons will allow me to overcome my challenges and live with integrity and wisdom. Imagine rating these qualities on a scale from "one-ten." Ten is the best, and one is the worst result. There is a negative and positive side to numerology. Up to this point in time I had been only supporting the negative lessons of my life according to my numerology. What did my life look like at that time? I was uncooperative and had difficulty doing anything in balance. I did not trust myself or anyone else, and I only shared what you wanted to hear so you would accept me. I didn't consider integrity, and I had no idea what wisdom was. This doesn't indicate that I was a bad person, but it defines the amount of struggle and frustration I was experiencing in life. I related to all of the negative aspects as described in "The Life You Were Born to Live". They were correct; it explained what I had been experiencing my entire life. What a great relief I felt because it gave me enough information and facts that I could start to examine my life more closely.

Here is how numerology works according to "The Life You Were Born to Live" by Dan Millman. Each of the numbers represents lessons you must learn, and the first two numbers (I am a 27/9) represent challenges on the way to learning your overall life lesson (My overall lesson is a "9"). The behaviors associated with our lessons all get woven together in what becomes a very intricate, confusing and misleading way to live life when we aren't aware of our individual lessons. Understanding the meaning of each number allows you to start to unravel your life lessons as they appear in your life. When looking at just one number and studying the effects of that lesson in your life, consider how it shows up. You will see repetitive issues that appear to be different in nature but are caused by the same lesson. Simple is better; take one step at a time and follow this path that will lead you to your blocks and blind spots. The lessons eventually get learned, as long as you are on the correct course. What is a lesson learned? You have awareness of the lesson, and whenever anything shows up in your life that embodies the energy of that lesson, you can make a different choice as a result of your awareness. The choice you make is your statement that this is a lesson learned.

The Life You Were Born to Live ~ Dan Millman

1. Creativity and Confidence

Bringing positive energy into the world.

2. Cooperation and Balance

Clarify the limits of your responsibility and learn to work

with others in a spirit of harmony, balance and mutual support.

3. Expression and Sensitivity

Utilize your emotional sensitivity to

bring heartfelt expression into the world.

4. Stability and Process

Achieve stability and security by patiently

following a gradual process toward selected goals.

5. Freedom and Discipline

Find more inner freedom through discipline,

focus and depth of expression.

6. Vision and Acceptance

You are here to reconcile your high ideals with practical

reality and to accept yourself, your world, and the present moment

through an expanded vision of life's inherent perfection.

7. Trust and Openness

You are here to trust the light or spirit within yourself, in others,

and in the process of your life so that you feel safe enough to

open up and share your inner beauty with the world.

8. Power and Abundance

You are here to work with abundance, power and recognition

and to apply your success to the common good.

9. Integrity and Wisdom

You are here to live in accord with your highest integrity,

to align your life with your heart's intuitive wisdom,

and to inspire others by example.

0. Inner Gifts

The zero does not have a life purposes as such, but rather

points to your inner gifts or potential resources.

The meanings of the numbers in numerology listed above are all the positive aspects each number. Our lessons will show up as behavior that does not represent the positive portion of our life lesson number. For example, someone that has "1" in their life lessons is going to struggle with confidence, and their creativity will be blocked or at least feel that way. For the time being, I am interested in the negative side of our life lessons because this provides specific information about our struggles and what is blocking us. When we understand what is blocking us, we can make choices that will lead directly to the positive aspects of our life lessons.

Here is an example: I am working with a client and their numerology is 26/8. I immediately know they have financial challenges. The 8 represents power and abundance, and with this life lesson, they are going to have difficulties with money and owning their power. They hired me as a coach to help them achieve their desires in life. Once I have done an empowerment assessment to determine what they feel is blocking them or standing in their way and holding them back, we start to examine resources that will take them to the other side of their challenges. This is when we review their Divine Gifts which activates their Divine Energy! At this time they are ready to make choices using their Divine Gifts which makes it very easy to make choices that support their true life purpose. It is difficult to deal with your lessons when you have no awareness of them! It is easy to get to the other side of your challenges as you are flowing the power of your Divinity, and you watch the challenges melt away.

I am going to discuss numerology in general and share with you what I have learned after working with hundreds of clients. I highly recommend that you buy "The Life You Were Born to Live" and learn what is blocking you from living your life purpose. I've had my copy for nearly 25 years, and I read it often. Why? Because each time I read it I gain more information about myself, what's blocking me, holding me back and standing in the way of living my true life purpose now. You must remember that we are alive, on earth and living with a handicap that is called our life lessons. The purpose is to improve our life and "The Life You Were Born to Live" will allow you to do that. If you study this book and learn how to get past all of your life lessons, you will be left with your Divine Gifts.

The information in the book is not exact, rather it is like a loose fitting garment. It doesn't predict your outcome. You make choices every day that affect your outcome. It is impossible to describe what your actual life will look like because there are too many physical influences that affect the outcome. Whenever you encounter a challenge and examine the source causing the problem, you will see how your life lessons are affecting you. The experience on your life path may seem different or appear different than someone else's experience with the same numbers. But we're only seeing what's happening with someone else from the outside, and all of our challenges have to do with how we feel inside and the stories that protect our feelings.

"Viewing our life purpose as a mountain path leads to an important discovery: Our life purpose - what we are here to do - is not what comes easiest."

— *Dan Millman, "The Life You Were Born to Live"*

Keep an open mind with the understanding that your purpose is to tap into your true potential in life. Any information you can obtain that will give you a higher level of awareness will allow you to make better choices. This information is going to show you, over time, how you fit into the big picture from a universal perspective. It allows you to explore your inner potential and all of your potential sits directly on the other side of your life lessons. Your life lessons are an integral part of your path to truth. If you want to create more order, form, and beauty in your life, it's mandatory that you learn what's blocking you from that. As you learn more about your lessons and make different choices, you clear space, energetically, that strengthens your connection to the flow of universal energy, intuition, a sense of purpose and your direction in life.

I continued to re-read "The Life You Were Born to Live" every month, and this gave me another realization. As I first read the portions that described my life, I was unable to connect with specific parts. As I read my numerology, I couldn't relate to some of the different aspects of my life lessons. What I learned over time through observation, was that every part pertained to me. I made new choices in life when I saw the blocks from my life lessons appear, and I gained more clarity and power. To begin with, I had many blind spots. In fact when I read about some of my lessons in the book I said, "No, that's not me!" When these aspects of my numerology that I couldn't initially relate to started to appear in my life, I started taking notice and gaining more awareness. Numerology is not an exact science, but it is quality information and, when examined over time, will explain all aspects of your life's challenges. For the first time in my life, I understood who I was, and it allowed me to make changes that had an immediate positive impact on my life. I knew my path of learning in life, and that allowed a much more powerful focus, choices, and results.

Examining my life from this perspective has taught me about who I was and who I am. When I examined the past what I discovered was I didn't have "me". I was too busy being what I thought would make other people like me. Or I was rebelling against what they said I should be or should do. I never had my authentic self and never would have my authentic self unless I woke up and made different choices. So I started making different options, and I used "The Life You Were Born to Live" as my guide into my real life. I tried many different approaches to change my life but got no difference in the results. The specific questions I wanted the answers to was, why I am so miserable? What is missing in me? Why do I feel that if people knew me, they wouldn't love me? Why don't I feel good enough? When will I ever feel satisfied that I have met the expectations of my parents, siblings, family, associates and my friends? It took me a long time to get to this realization because these same sacred beliefs that no longer served my evolution were making decisions for me, moment by moment, day in and day out. They were advising me during my transformation. I was going to the source of the problem and asking for the solution. So I started my reconstruction process and discovered not only was my life out of control, but I didn't even have a life of my own.

Using numerology to point out where my blocks were going to appear, I was able to start identifying many of the obstacles immediately as they appeared. This awareness allowed me to see that everyone has life lessons and part of the challenge is dealing with many issues at work, home or socially that are caused by intersecting life lessons with myself and the relationships in my life. I quickly realized that the only person I could change was me, and I was only responsible for myself. What helps others the most is "me" living at the highest vibration possible. Understanding my life lessons allows me to make choices that take me to a higher vibration. Understanding your numerology, even a minimal amount of experience, will assist you in life immediately. Some of your confrontations, disagreements, and disruptions seem baffling until you understand numerology and your life lessons.

So let's look at some of the areas that are blocking us so we can gain more awareness about our obstacles. It is the awareness of these obstacles that will allow us to make a choice that supports our self-actualization. As we encounter our life lessons, they are a disruption that generates fear and upset in our life at the moment. Our life lessons can intimidate and scare us or leave us baffled, angry, frustrated, lonely and exhausted when we have no awareness of them. One thing with life lessons everyone has in common is this: we all have lessons to learn, and the lesson is not going to go away even when we have learned it! Our life lessons continue to appear again and again until we face it, learn it, heal it and then love it because our life lessons will always be with us while we are on earth. They diminish in strength as we become more aware of our lessons and continue to love them and thank them for our learning.

Your life is always part of the energetic flow of the universe, and you will be given opportunities by the universe that will allow you to learn and heal your life lessons. The universe creates events in your life that are designed to get your attention. Maybe it's a fender-bender with your car, not getting a job you applied for, an illness, a pain in your neck or a sore back. It could be anything, but it definitely will be a disruption to the flow of your life. This is how the universe speaks to get your attention when you are unconscious. Each time the universe provides the opportunity for you to learn more about your life lessons, it does so with a little more volume and strength. Ignore the message from the universe and the size or impact will increase the next time the universe speaks. When I was living unconsciously, I was associating these events with "bad luck." When is the other shoe going to fall? Why does this always happen to me? It was the universe trying to get my attention, and I didn't realize it.

Your perceptions and memories of what happened while you were growing up are your own. Whatever you think or believe is your interpretation, and your stories have a tendency to change as more time passes, and they seem to grow in strength. The stories inside you about your past assisted you in your quest for survival at a very young age. However, those stories, beliefs, and perceptions may not serve you at this time in your life. They may not be in alignment with your life today and are affecting the choices you make in each moment. How you felt at that time of your life was real, but the stories that create these feelings may not be. Over the course of time, these stories gain strength and build more intense emotions. You may get confused about life and lose your real purpose. "The Life You Were Born to Live" will guide you back to your true path. You have an opportunity to write a new story, something that will support who you truly are as you live your life purpose. It is time to start a new chapter!

Some people have had horrific childhoods, while others would say they came from the best family anyone could imagine. Both are affected by their upbringing which is influenced by your perceptions, which are determined by your life lessons. When you are here to learn a lesson and you live in survival your view of the world is going to be how to protect yourself. There were things learned and beliefs created that no longer serve the expansion of our souls. Acquiring an understanding of these beliefs proves that we no longer have to be controlled by the events of our past. In both cases, there are life lessons to be learned, and if we want tomorrow to look different from today, we have to make different choices and take different actions now.

For example, I was speaking to a client who was angry and upset. I told him that anger wasn't serving him, it was destroying him. He told me that having anger in that situation was part of his Latin culture! He was right; it was part of his Latin Culture because that is what he chose. It was a rationalization that gave him permission to stay angry! Everyone has stories and beliefs from childhood, and we live our lives based on the stories we protect. Our stories are our reconstruction of past events in life designed to protect us in survival, prove a point or reach a projected outcome, all in defense of the action and person who has taught us the story. What stories do you have? What are they protecting? What would your life look like without the story? When was the last time you told the story? How often do you find yourself defending your stories and beliefs? I had a lot of stories that I had made up in my head, and some of them were pretty wild. Over time we tend to embellish our stories and build more and more protection for ourselves!

I have never had a problem being successful; my challenge was holding on to the success. I would sabotage myself or get bored and move on to something new. This happened repeatedly, and I never understood why I behaved that way, doing the same thing again and again and expecting different results. Looking back, it was a loop that repeated itself many times. Each time the story was different, the players were different, and the location was different, but the results were very similar. I got locked into very subtle patterns of behavior that assured I would get the same results! As I look back now, I can see that I didn't have control of my life. Even though I was successful, creative and working hard, I eventually created the same situation over and over again. Deep inside I knew something was missing; there was no sense of fulfillment. I knew that if I built a business empire and became a billionaire that feeling would still be there and it seemed to be growing a little more each day. I was putting the proper amount of attention, time, hard work and discipline into my career but the results were not adding up. Life was a struggle and needed distractions that would take me away from my internal discomfort.

We have been making decisions based on who we aren't. That's what we do; we do what we believe is the correct thing to do. But a majority of the time we are told by someone else what the right thing to do is. It may not be right for us because it doesn't support our true life purpose. You may not be getting the results you desire, or you have an empty feeling that won't go away. We continually try different ways to get rid of the feeling but it never really seems to work. Of course not, we are making decisions based on information that is faulty. If you were going bake a chocolate cake, you wouldn't add chicken broth instead of milk or water, would you? Maybe I will use mustard for the frosting! If you don't have a recipe and you are trying to create something using the wrong ingredients, your results are going to be disappointing. In the same way, it is difficult to support your life purpose as you apply incorrect information passed on to you from someone else's belief system and influenced by your perceptions of survival.

I knew I couldn't live a life up to the standards that were demand-ed by my parents and the Catholic Church. I was going down the wrong path in life, but that didn't bother me, I knew it and accepted it. I was re-bellious, and that creates an "I could care less" attitude about life. The path led me in a loop of the same actions and the same results for many years. Now I know why; I kept making my past become my future. The best we can do is recreate the past unless we take entirely new actions which will undoubtedly create different results. Our minds are very tricky by nature. As we use our mind, we can only resource past experiences composed of previous impressions, feelings, reactions, and interpretations. If ten people were asked to draw a picture of a house with trees, flowers and a white picket fence, everyone's perception would be different. Each of the ten people has had different experiences in their past, and this will be obvi-ous in their artwork. We do the same thing every time we are looking for information, especially when making plans for the future. Pretend your past is a long, narrow carpet lying on the ground behind you. You pick up the end of the carpet with your hands and you are facing to the future with the carpet draped off your shoulders like a cape. Now, snap the carpet over your head and lay it out neatly, directly in front of you so you can walk into your future. That is only a re-creation of past experiences and will create the same results again and again.

Nothing seemed to fill the emptiness I felt inside. I was never happy; something always felt as though it was missing for most of my life. When I accomplished something, it didn't satisfy me and I still felt incomplete. How could I feel whole and complete? I was making my choices based on faulty information. I was in survival, only focused on my physical needs. I was going in the wrong direction. I satisfied my Body and Mind, but not my Spirit. Life is really about how we handle all of the disruptions and interruptions each day. With each choice we declare which direction we are choosing; to remain in conflict or rise above it. The unexpected events that keep appearing are going to ignite the lessons we are here to learn. The universe is giving us many opportunities to grow.

Have you ever driven down the highway and arrived at your destination and remember little or nothing about how you got there? Where were you during that time? There is such a fine line between living in our (un)conscious state of mind and being in a state of hypnosis. I believe we live many portions of our lives that way, on autopilot, as if we were hypnotized. I know that I do. I am a very conscious person and yet I still find myself operating on autopilot. There is always room for improvement. We are human, and we each go through our stages of evolution. Being conscious is a full-time commitment; it requires that we are connected to our hearts and the hearts of others. It is easy to be led astray as we are moving down our Spiritual paths. There are many distractions and challenges in life. With each new choice

I make to support my Soul's expansion I move towards new experiences. Having "The Life You Were Born to Live" on my desk allows me to reference my challenges and make new choices that yield powerful results.

"If gravity is the glue that holds the universe together, balance is the key that unlocks the secrets. All things exist in a state of balance.."

— *Dan Millman*

The unknown is what brings excitement to my life, knowing that there is another area of Spiritual exploration for me to experience. We are Spiritual Beings having a physical experience, and the purpose is to learn our life lessons. As a result, we are always encountering other people who continually trigger our life lessons through our interactions with them. It has the appearance that others are creating stress, disruptions, problems, chaos, and confusion in our lives. The truth is that we are energetically attracting our life lessons to us and our perceptions of our interaction will come from our life lessons unless we make new choices. These situations are all brought to us to allow us to learn more about ourselves, our life lessons, to heal and to choose to transform our lives. There are enough choices made by other people around us that have a direct effect on our lives, by causing disruption, chaos, confusion and a wide variety of different effects from their life lessons. Rather than making choices that will add to the mess, we can make a new choice that benefits our personal growth.

When we eliminate ourselves as a source of disturbance, we create space for the development of new perceptions. Awareness creates power; it allows us to make compelling choices that will improve our life in an instant. That is the beauty of our non-physical energy; the results are immediate. we don't have to practice, just make a choice that supports the expansion of our soul and we get instant results. One of the easiest ways to do this is to carefully examine our sacred beliefs and look for opinions that we feel we must protect and see how that belief is generated from or supported by our life lessons.

These beliefs have been twisted and distorted over the years as they have filtered through the family tree. No wonder there is so much behavior in the world that is hard to comprehend. In essence, throughout your childhood, you learned from your parents how they handled difficult situations; it was the best they could come up with based on their upbringing, their sacred beliefs and the depth of their survival-based lifestyle. If your parents had a lot of fear, you would be heavily influenced by that energy. Throughout the ages, many beliefs have been passed on and taught that are not true. The closer you examine the belief systems you were taught, the less truth you will find. Truth is a moving target; it is typically loaded with predetermined objectives or is distorted by your opinions, sacred beliefs, and your level of survival. Truth is subjective, and yet you were taught to behave a certain way based on the foundation of truth that was taught to you as a child.

Why are there untruths being represented as Truth? Because there is a motive (expectation) associated with the proposed truth. Even if you had a "perfect" childhood, there are sacred beliefs that are blocking you from self-actualization and living your true life purpose. Your parents were trying to raise a family to provide food and shelter and care for the children as best they could. When they got alarmed because something happened or something was said, your parents responded immediately to their sacred beliefs and the influence of their life lessons. Everything your parents taught you was the best way they had learned to respond to any situation. Here are some of the common comments; "No use crying over spilled milk,"Money doesn't grow on trees,"Children should be seen and not ...." (I know you can finish the sentence). There is an endless list of these sacred beliefs and they do not serve the expansion of your soul.

Sacred beliefs are stored at the core of our cellular memory. They are engrained in our being and are part of us at a core physical level. This explains our collective experience of telling our children something and realizing we are making the same statements that our parents made to us. We are repeating these statements for the same reason; wanting to maintain control of the household. At that moment, we are looking for a way to control our child's behavior, and we instinctively respond and say something based on our internal sacred beliefs.

I watched a woman interacting with her son this way in the super-market. She had told him to stop picking up something on the shelf, but he didn't stop. She put her hands on her hips, looked at him squarely and start-ed to count slowly."One, two..." The child responded before she reached number three. Sound familiar? This parent-child relationship cycle has been perpetuated for centuries from generation to generation. In many instances, these beliefs are so deeply embedded that people don't even recognize that they are being influenced by them, to the point of losing control of their life. But it isn't just our parents; let's look at some of the other areas where we learn these sacred beliefs, such as all of the people, places and things in your life that influenced you as a child. Your family, neighbors, babysitters, teachers, clergy, the geographic area, your neighborhood, the economic con-ditions and countless other factors all influenced your sacred beliefs.

Start with your family; brothers, sisters, cousins, nieces, nephews, aunts, uncles, grandparents and great-grandparents and look at each of these people in your life and see what interactions you had and how they affect you today. I have been in very intimate personal transformation seminars where a brother and sister have shared their own stories, and it sounded like they lived in two different homes in two different areas of the world. Someone from the West Coast shared, and it seemed like they lived in my house on the East Coast. We all have life lessons and misperceptions about what is really happening in our lives because we are responding based on our inner beliefs.

The day that we're born, we enter the world with life lessons. Imagine for a moment the influence these lessons had on our perceptions as a child. When we are dependent on somebody else to take care of us from birth, our opinions about our caretakers get tainted due to the life lessons that we are here to learn. The influence of these experiences affects us throughout our life and in many instances, are controlling us to this day. By learning about our life lessons through numerology, we can start to get an understanding of how these lessons are affecting our life. It is a lifelong process because our lessons are always with us. Each time you make a choice that supports your self-actualization and your true life purpose you gain more control of your life. The more you acknowledge your lessons, let them know you appreciate how they protected you in the past. Their strength continues to diminish, your awareness continues to grow, and you start to create more peace, joy, and love in your life.

Have you ever heard that anything that bothers us about another person is a reflection of what is bothering us inside? This is entirely accurate and an excellent way to get in-depth information about what is causing upsets and disturbances in your life. The world is a mirror, and the only thing we see in the world is a reflection of us. Realizing that I was always seeing a reflection of me helped me change my behaviors rapidly. If I am angry, I see anger; if I am humble, I see humility. Whatever I see is a reflection of me. Why is this true? Let's look at the process involved. You see something that upsets you, or maybe you make a negative or judgmental statement about what you just saw or heard. You processed what you saw through your mind. Your mind is a tool that can resource our past experiences and your past experiences determine what you see and how you feel. When you look at something that bothers you, what you are witnessing is your interpretation based on your experience. Everything you see in the world is a reflection of you. When you accept and utilize this teaching, it is a sure-fire way to understand what's blocking you, standing in your way or holding you back from living a self-actualized life living your true purpose. Who is in your life now, and what are you seeing happen in your world is all a reflection of you.

Many times people have told me that they read "The Life You Were Born to Live" but they didn't connect with much of what it said about their life lessons. This is caused by blind spots and a possible unwillingness to look at oneself honestly. When you have spent your life protecting yourself and wanting to be "happy" you develop a tendency to avoid your short comings. Your objective when you read the portion of Dan Millman's book that applies to you is to find "why it applies and how it applies" in your life. Qualify yourself, don't disqualify yourself. You have been taught to protect your beliefs and to protect your beliefs is creating a life of resistance. This is why I continue to read "the Life You Were Born to Live" frequently. It is imperative because when you have blind spots, something you are unaware of will reveal itself over time.

What amazed me was to see that over a 20 year period studying numerology and my life lessons, I still have blind spots. This is part of our evolutionary process as we continue to grow. As we continue to grow, we uncover more information about out life lessons that allow us to increase our level of self-actualization. With each level of growth, we keep repeating this process. New life lessons continue to appear; maybe I should say the same old life lessons appear with an entirely different look to them. The experience may seem different at first, but as we research the cause, we will continue to find the same old beliefs that don't serve us anymore. The ego likes to stay in action. Any opportunity that we unconsciously give the ego is allowing the ego to have its way and control us. When we're conscious and in a constant state of creating new awareness, the ego quiets down.

Numerology is the most powerful resource available to us! We are living life on earth, right now. We must stay connected to our physical reality, learn our life lessons and transcend them (with energy) into our life purpose. Staying focused on our life lessons keeps us grounded, and that is important. Stay grounded and allow the energy to come to you, don't go out to the energy. Anyone that is familiar with energy through meditation or other spiritual practices, knows they release themselves from the physical and experience different forms of bliss. These practices are meaningful and will enhance anyone's spiritual journey. But we must return to our life in the physical and allow as much Divine Energy as possible flow through us. It's all about our lessons here on earth. As we flow our Divine Energy into our life, we are living life in the most potent form possible. When we interact with people on a daily basis, our energy will be refreshing and provide a new mirror for others who desire more from life.

"The Life You Were Born to Live" provides us with new perceptions every time we refer back to Dan Millman's book. With each layer of lessons we learn, our life changes significantly. It is a continual process of learning our lessons in life. Each cleansing we activate through our choices allows us to live our life purpose at a higher energetic level. All of our lessons are "life lessons," and our purpose is to stay grounded on earth and transcend our lessons so we may be of higher service to others. We are in the midst of our life, and the more we focus on gaining an understanding of our life lessons, the faster we will move into higher levels of self-actualization.

Your ego is always going to lead in the direction it desires; your heart is going to lead down the path of truth, your truth.

Guideposts for Your Journey.

1. Gaining awareness of your life lessons allows you to make better choices that will improve your life each day. What is something you learned about yourself and your life lesson that will enable you to make better choices?

2. Can you identify any of your sacred beliefs that are no longer serving you? What is one choice you can make that will improve your life today?

3. What do other people do that bothers you? How is that a reflection of you? Today remain aware that the world is a mirror and identify three attributes others have that you are identifying with. How will these improve your life?

CHAPTER FIVE ~ Transcendence

As a child, I never really had the luxury of choice in my life. I was living my life entirely in response to the people's reaction around me. I was struggling with life and not understanding it, which made me very reactionary to other people's words and actions. I was always in a defensive mode, protecting myself, my inadequacies and my fear of life itself. I had no choice; I knew no other options. I was trying to survive, the best I could, hoping no one noticed how lost I felt. I now realize that many people felt the same way. Last year I did a survey on being stressed and overwhelmed, and 25 people volunteered to take the study. The overwhelming majority of people were deeply troubled by stress and overwhelm in their life. The degree of stress and overwhelm varied but the way everyone felt on the inside was very similar. They each had a feeling of lack of self-worth and also felt hopeless about a resolution to the problem. The most surprising thing that happened was their transparency, sharing in great detail and depth their innermost feelings. I sensed that they felt relieved having the opportunity to speak honestly about how they felt, with a compassionate, empathetic person to listen. I was amazed at how this experience affected me; it made me more committed to getting my message out to a much broader audience. I wish I had a magic wand that I could wave.

Did you ever wish you had a magic wand? Maybe a wand like a fairy godmother used in the Wizard of Oz or a magic lantern that you found on the beach, and when you rubbed it a genie appeared? Do you remember those childhood fantasies? You were free to be as creative as you desired and everyone thought it was cute because you were a kid. It is acceptable for children but not for adults! You were conditioned to meld into your family, society, culture, and your geographic conditions. No time for magic wands not when you are focused on survival. Life is about learning to "fit in," be accepted and get approval from those around us. What if you could still use that magic wand today? What would you do with it?

Let's find that answer right now. Sit back, close your eyes, take a breath, let go of your life today and connect with your child-like imagination for a few minutes.

How was that experience for you? Were you able to connect with your childlike imagination? Or maybe you are blocked, or you immediately thought "this is stupid". Either way, I can understand because we feel that type of behavior is not acceptable as an adult. What if I told you that I could connect you to a magic wand; would you believe me? You each have powers that can provide the same results, but snuff out this belief because it does not fit into the mindset of a survival society! Self-actualization is not supported by survival either. In fact, it is the exact opposite of surviving - it is thriving! Do you want to use a magic wand or continue to be controlled by the people, places, and things around you? I am going to show you how to reactivate your magic wand! It is called transcendence, and it works just like a magic wand. When you use this power, magic happens. You don't get to control the outcome, you activate the process by transcending energy, and then you get to sit back and watch the magic happen.

Transcendence is an experience that is beyond the normal or physical level of existence. When we transcend we are only working with energy, a vibration and we influence the vibrational field with the energy behind our thoughts, words, and actions. We ignite the process and the universe steps in and handles the fulfillment of the results. We can intend for the physical results but we can't control the outcome. Our position is to ignite and support the process energetically and remain detached from the results. Authentic power is an energetic expression of our Divine Gifts coming into physical form when we are in service to others. Authentic power is an ultra-high-frequency energy that fuels and accelerates transcendence. What is taking place in the physical world is not essential. What is important is our perception of the world and the quality of our intentions. The only thing wrong with the world is our perception of it. When we learn to detach from the world as a whole, we can focus on our intentions and the energy we are contributing to the world; our life becomes much more meaningful.

We live in a physical world that is based on survival, hunting, gathering and measuring our success by material gain. We forget that the only path to authentic self-fulfillment is through our hearts. Feelings are the most accurate guideposts, and they are our primary means of communicating with our non-physical command center, our heart. Our hearts are the doorway to our soul. It is through feelings and energy that we have the most meaningful experiences in life. It isn't what happened; it is always about how we felt about the experience. When we focus on generating a loving energy in any situation in life, the results are going to improve.

**"If you only have a hammer,
you see every problem as a nail."**

— *Abraham Maslow*

To live your life purpose (self-actualization) at the highest level, you must understand energy and transcendence. You have the power to change any situation in life by using your ability to create authentic energy that is supportive and for the good of all involved. As you understand more about your authentic self-expression, you live life with more passion, purpose and heartfelt connection with everyone in your life. You are generating authentic power with your Divine Gifts, and anyone that gets near you feels the energy and believe me, they like it! It's actually kind of funny because when people feel your authentic power they don't know what it is but they know they feel good.

It is an inside game! What is happening with your "inner game" is what determines how you are going to react energetically to physical events in your life. The energy of emotions fuels your response to any situation in life. Your decision to act is determined (it will be a conditioned response) by the story and beliefs that support the emotion you are feeling. It is this energy that determines how you are going to act and speak as you respond to events around you that affect your life. Transcendence allows you to make a different internal choice and create new energy, one that is more supportive and loving.

What is transcendence? The definition of transcendence is existence or experience beyond the normal or physical level. Transcendence speaks specifically to our non-physical lives. We live in two dimensions, the physical and the non-physical. A life lived only in the physical without accessing the non-physical guarantees that we will live a life of servitude. We will be limiting ourselves to our hopeless reality of survival. The non-physical dimension is where access to authentic power resides. It is simple to access and available to everyone, everywhere and it is free!

Follow the blueprint and use the resources that I am sharing and you will have the freedom and control that you desire in your life. The next step is to start eliminating "stuff" that is not supporting your choice to live your life purpose. This is a moment by moment process, for each thought, word, and action determines your level of success. It is impossible to access your true life purpose without understanding how to allow the non-physical to flow through your physical Life.

When we live a life based on survival, we use the same techniques to resolve every situation. We are always seeking remedies that will be in our favor so that we can win and survive at a higher level of physical existence. It is a life focused on fulfilling our physical needs without authentic power on the inside because physical items will never provide authentic personal power or fulfillment. Abraham Maslow realized this, and towards the end of his life, he expanded the Hierarchy of Needs to include two more levels to accommodate the characteristics required to move towards transcendence, cognitive and aesthetic needs. Abraham Maslow realized that it is essential that we break away from the effects that our physical culture and physical environment have on our personal growth.

Self-fulfillment is the elusive goal that people chase, believing that more accomplishment(s) in the physical (material) world will fulfill the desired effect of self-fulfillment, but it never does. Success comes and goes, leaving us with a feeling that something is missing. Self-fulfillment is not external; it is at the core of our "inner game." We'll never get the satisfaction we're seeking from our external accomplishments. It is a non-physical (universal) perspective, not a physical perspective that's required to achieve self-fulfillment.

My experience from my transformation and working with hundreds of different clients is that we get stuck in "survival mode" and believe that this is life. There is so much more to life than survival! We are afraid to change or move in a new direction because it will upset a lifestyle that we are now protecting. There is nothing to protect! By following the guidelines in this book and gaining more awareness about the non-physical, we can create everything we desire right where we are now. We consider a new possibility, and we immediately block it because we don't know "how" to make it happen. We get stopped before we get started! "How" is the supreme killer of every dream in the world. I have personally experienced being blocked because I didn't know how! What I have come to learn is to focus on "what's next" and take one step. You don't need to know how, you simply need to know what your intention is and feed it positive, powerful, authentic energy from your heart and your dream will chase you down and jump into your lap! Regardless of your current situation, you can create anything you desire. To experience these majestic parts of life, it is necessary to understand the non-physical part of life and all of the resources that are available to us from the universe.

The process of transcendence uses a holistic perception, which is best for all involved. Follow the high road? How can my presence improve this situation? Maybe I am simply going to sit in support, peacefully creating calm, loving energy. When sharing I am always offering information that is the best for all and not only in support of my personal opinion. Even when I am reminded of a dramatic situation from my past, and I am feeling the fear generated from that experience, I choose to speak with love and transcend my fear. Transcendence is a choice, a choice to live at a higher vibration internally and supporting our intention with our thoughts, words, and actions.

Metaphysics (the non-physical) is an area that intimidates people because it requires a perspective that is contrary to the view of a survival reality. Very few people that I have worked with have understood metaphysics. I always ask my client to describe their understanding of metaphysics; this question always generates an instant response of silence! Then I typically hear this response "I am not able to answer the question." People are afraid to venture into the metaphysical world and share it with others for fear of ridicule from people around them. Metaphysics is referred to as "Woo-Woo" by people. Or it is referred to as "New Age Thinking," which is funny because there is nothing new about the non-physical, other than learning how crucial it is to us. The concepts in this book have been in existence since the beginning of the universe. Metaphysics operates the universe. Let that sink in, because we see everything from our physical reality which is extremely limited as we get consumed by survival in the physical world. But the world as we know it is planet earth, and the universe created the earth and established the operating instructions, which still apply today, and they are all non-physical.

I had the same experience as I went through my transformation. I was afraid to speak up because people were fixated on survival and they would verbally ridicule and discredit me and metaphysics. As time went on, I couldn't hide the fact that I was living an entirely different life and my guidelines for thriving came to the surface. As time went on it didn't matter to me anymore because my quality of life was wonderful. I stopped caring what people said and made a more profound commitment to my transformation. The exciting part of following this path is that every day you can make better choices because of new awareness of the previous day's experience. Each day you can create more an even higher vibration, more energy, more power, and more personal fulfillment.

"If you want to find the secrets of the Universe, think in terms of energy, frequency, and vibration."

— Nicholas Tesla

In the physical world, we each live in our reality. Each person has a perception of what they see and hear based on their life experiences. Everyone has had different past life experiences; we come from different families, different environments, and different cultures which have all contributed to our core beliefs. Our realities are different, and as we experience our lives on a daily basis, we are profoundly affecting the expectations and results of anyone we encounter by our energy. We live in a competitive environment with winners and losers, which is a survival based perception. We get trapped in the survival game, and we never get out of the first three levels of needs, because we are stuck competing for our basic survival needs. It is a continuous loop that plays over-and-over again in our lives. Our evolution is dependent upon accessing universal resources. Transcendence requires that we utilize all the resources of the universe, not just the physical survival tools on earth. Are you aware of all the resources the universe has to offer?

We live on earth, which is one of the planets that make up our solar system. The universe created our solar system, and the universe has an operating guide that is omnipotent. By just understanding the basic operating structure of the universe you can change your life quickly and easily. The universe has seven fundamental laws that operate everything in the universe. When we become aware of these and begin to implement these in our lives, we will immediately see where we can transcend our energy to improve our lives. Universal resources are available to all of us, free of charge if we choose to use them to create a more fulfilling life. I refer to them as resources because when we use them, they always bring significant improvement to our lives. If we don't choose them consciously, then we won't be in the flow of the universal energy, and we will probably be in resistance to the flow of energy. The universal laws are "in play" 100% of the time, and your lack of awareness doesn't mean they aren't having an impact on your life. The universe is always in motion, creating, and flowing energy, and the universe is always about expansion. When we let go of our self-importance and how we protect our beliefs that support a survival lifestyle we can use these resources to create a life that is unimaginable to us now.

If I told you that you could live a life beyond your wildest dreams and it only requires that you do one thing, would you do it? The only thing you have to do is understand the seven universal laws and apply them in your life. I assure you that as you learn them, you will see that they are already operating in your life, and you are not consciously choosing them to enhance your life. There is a high probability that you are in resistance to these seven laws due to lack of awareness. It is part of the fabric of your struggles in life. Everything we learned at a young age was survival; we weren't taught about the universal laws. Because of this we only learned how to behave and act in a manner that was approved by the authority figures in our childhood. We were taught to fit in!

The universe only knows abundance and operates directly from seven laws and, when you align yourself with the universe, you have the power of these laws working for you. When you are using the universal laws consciously, you are in alignment with the cosmos (all that is). Being in alignment with the cosmos allows heaven (non-physical) and earth (physical) to unify in a way that yields magical results. This is the zone of creativity where you can powerfully and majestically manifest something from nothing! You just need to plant the seed of intention in the fertile energy of universal resources and water the seed with the energy of your thoughts, words, and actions. The energy of your intention is required to start the process but your choices each day determine the outcome. It is necessary to create energy in support of your intentions as you go through your day. This is the key to successful manifestation.

What are the Universal Laws? There are seven universal laws; the first three are fixed, they cannot be changed. But the last four are influenced directly by your energy, and you can transcend them with energy. Let's review the universal laws:

The first three Universal Laws are unchangeable:

The Law of Mentalism: Everything is part of the Universal Mind, a single consciousness. Everything we experience in the physical world had its origin in the invisible space known as the universe. Simply stated, "Everything comes from nothing."

The Law of Correspondence: As above, so below. Yin, and Yang. We are body, mind, and spirit and all is one, and all is in agreement. There is harmony, cooperation, and connection among everything created, regardless of the dimension in which it resides.

The Law of Vibration: Everything is a vibration. Nothing is static; everything is always in a constant state of change including your body, your mind, and your spirit. Everything is always in motion and like energy attracts like energy. Our energy attracts or repels other energies.

The four alterable Universal Laws are:

The Law of Polarity: Everything has opposites (Yin/Yang). There are two sides to everything: love and hate, hot and cold, happy and sad, positive, and negative. Each is, in fact, the same thing to a differing degree.

The Law of Rhythm: What goes out must come in, what goes up must come down. You witness the Law of Rhythm in all aspects of life. The pendulum swings both ways an equal distance from one side to the other.

The Law of Cause and Effect: Every cause has an effect, and every effect has a cause. Our intention facilitates the cause and is a powerful way to create, the results of your intention in physical form are the effect. The universe will show you precisely through your results how you formed your intention (cause).

The Law of Gender: Everything has masculine and feminine qualities. It is the recognition and expression of these qualities that make us whole. It allows us to maintain balance in our lives and our perceptions of others.

The fixed Universal Laws are the ingredients that make your foundation; everything comes from nothing, everything vibrates, your body, mind, and spirit are all aligned with your energy. It is essential to recognize the role the universal laws play in your true life purpose. Everything in the universe is a vibration and your Divine Gifts are a vibrating energy. The universal laws are the super highway that your Divine Gifts flow through. These Laws will lead you to your Divinity and will always be in support of your true life purpose, always! To get there, however, you must recognize all of the things that are blocking your path. As you figure out what blocks you and you step to the other side of the challenge, you open space for more energy to flow. Then you will be able to access and use the seven universal laws with more energy and manifest better and better results. The universe works in mysterious ways, but it never operates from fear. The universe is only based on love and expansion, and when you get in alignment with the universe, you will have the most powerful resources available in "your corner" supporting you. When you are aligned with the universe, you will understand the meaning of creation, contentment, and love. How you perceive and experience it is determined by your choices and your perception of life because the energetic results become self-evident instantly.

"Transcendence refers to the very highest and most inclusive or holistic levels of human consciousness, behaving and relating, as ends rather than means, to oneself, to significant others, to human beings in general, to other species, to nature, and to the cosmos."

— *"The Farther Reaches of Human Nature"* ~ *Abraham Maslow*

The universe can't say no! It is required to deliver to us everything that we request. I found this hard to believe it first. Why was I experiencingso much struggle in a universe that flows so abundantly? I was struggling because I learned to live in limitation. My thoughts, words, and actions of lack did not support the universe; they blocked the universe from delivering to me. I am the one who keeps me down. I am the one who does not allow. I am the one who does not feel good enough to bathe in the magnificence that the universe has to offer. This is how I learned to perceive life as a child. The smallest sacred belief can prevent you from the grandeur of life. The hero's journey is the journey into your heart, into your feelings and connecting with your soul. The more you do this, and the deeper you go into the depth of your soul, the more you will be able to experience unconditional love.

We have a physical reality that we define with our five senses, and our metaphysical reality gets expressed through our energy. It is a reality of feelings, energy, and vibration. This is the energy that connects us with the universe; it is the source of the energy we infuse into everything we think, say and do. The universe responds to our energy (vibration) based on the energy we are transmitting; it uses no logic, it merely responds "in-kind" to our vibration. The more we understand how to raise our vibration the more significant our connection to the universe will be and the greater our results.

There are two sides to the road of life - the physical side and the non-physical side. To achieve self-actualization, we must drive down the center of the path of life. It is in this manner that we can be connected to both dimensions at the same time. By integrating the non-physical (spiritual) into our physical reality, we are significantly enhancing our life. Once we start choosing to look at every aspect of our life from a non-physical perspective, we immediately began to transition away from survival. We are part of the universe, and each of us individually generates our frequency and these frequencies, which in turn, attract our experiences in life. What energies are you producing; survival, competition and fear, or energy cooperation, abundance and love?

Awareness is the key to your success. To make significant changes that lead to self-actualization and your true life purpose, you must learn about the tools and resources that allow you to live such a powerful life. The thing that I find so fascinating is how quickly people learn and make new choices that change their lives instantly. As you connect to these resources, it awakens your spirit, and you naturally understand the path to follow. You have been making decisions based on who you aren't, while you struggle for survival. It's not your fault; it is how you were taught, and you live in a self-policing society that demands conformity. When you start to understand the universe, you begin to understand yourself because you are an integral part of the universe. The transition is rapid because once you acknowledge non-physical energy, you start to transcend your life into self-actualization. This is who you are as a Spiritual being; you have an energy that is connected directly to universal energy, and you are part of all that is.

Here is how I would define spirituality from a metaphysical per-spective. Spirituality: as relating to, or affecting the human spirit or soul as opposed to material or physical things; the quality of being concerned with the human spirit or soul as opposed to material or physical things. *http://www.dictionary.com/browse/spiritual*

Many people associate to spirituality being religious, and while this is also true, it only applies to the physical world! There is no religion in the non-physical world; it is a world of energy. In the physical, there are many different religions each with distinctive doctrines, yet still supported entirely by the universal Laws. You will quickly see how the universal description of spirituality can easily apply to any religion. Learning how to become self-actualized will not interfere with any religion, rather it will enhance your entire life experience including your religious beliefs. Spirituality has a common ground that supports everyone choosing what is best for the evolution of their soul. It is an individual choice for each person to make and, as a spiritual being, I treat your choice with reverence and respect.

As we start to understand the common universal thread that connects everything, we will learn that by applying a universal perspective to our lives we find our path much more comfortable to follow and our experiences start to gain more significance. Our lives in the past contained struggle, stress and worry as we did our best to live each day correctly. When we look at life without the universe involved, we become a pawn in someone else's game! If we aren't building our dreams, we are building someone else's dream! It is a life where we measure ourselves against others to determine how well we are doing based on everyone else's expectations and results. So much of our experience has been centered in resistance, either resisting those who control us or following directives given to us, and living in resistance to the universal flow of energy. It becomes a delicate balancing act because the universe is always in motion, and we are either flowing with the energy of the universe, or we are static and in resistance to it. It is all about energy, not our mindset but the flow of energy. Once we experience using universal energy, we will adjust our mindset to support our choice. Currently, we change our mindset in attempting to get better results, without using universal resources, and this can only lead to confusion, struggle and frustration.

Coaches work with the mindset and get clients to take on new perceptions by going through different processes designed by the coach to achieve the results desired. This creates resistance because changing our mind does not allow us to be in unison with the flow of Universal energy, it only allows us to take different actions which may or may not be supportive to our self-actualization and true life purpose. The metaphysical world is only concerned with energy, and the source of energy is our heart. At this time when we speak of mindset, we are referring to changing our attitude. It is mandatory that we stop using our mind to find the solution, as our mind only refers to the

146

past, and we already know the results following that path. To transcend, we must connect to and start speaking from our heart! It is how we feel that will determine the energetic vibration or resonance we are transmitting, not our mindset. Our mind uses logic and our heart generates energy.

Our feelings guide us to universal energy, and our heart is the mechanism that generates our energy. Universal energy is always flowing through us; without it, we have no "Life Force" and we no longer exist in the physical. As we experience our feelings it is important to flow them, don't hang on to them, let them flow! E-motions are simply energy in motion. We can respond in kind to the energy as it relates to our physical reality or we can respond to the powerful energy of the non-physical. This is where we get stuck in the lower levels of the "Hierarchy of Needs"; we have feelings that we are not flowing. We have stories attached to our feelings, stories that have been part of us for decades and also they involve our physical experience. Change our story, change our life! When we get stuck in the physical aspect of life, we need only choose to allow the powerful energy of the universe to flow through us. As we continue to learn more about the Universal resources, we can use these laws to transcend anything, and it only takes three elements: awareness, free will, and choice. With these three things, we can transcend anything.

A new client that I was working with had a rental property that had become "the rental property from hell." Every time they thought about the property, they were fearful and they believed there would be continual problems. The history of their ownership, the tenants and the physical issues with the property gave them substantial justification for their feelings. What they wanted to do was get rid of the property, but they believed they would have a tough time selling it. Their entire perception of the property was based on their experience, but it was in resistance to their initial intentions of making a solid investment. The physical experience got the best of them. The moment they told me about the situation and I saw their energetic vibration as it related to the property, I stopped them immediately so that we could talk about how they felt about the property. My client got visibly upset and had nothing good to say about the entire situation. I showed my client how the energy they were generating was creating more problems! I taught them how to transcend their feelings and take energetic actions to improve the situation. We created an affirmation that "the perfect buyer for this property will purchase the property." Rather than continue with the stress, financial anxiety and overall negative perception regarding the property, we chose to create positive energy through an affirmation that stated that the perfect buyer would buy the property. In the meantime, there was nothing to do except create more positive energy and wait.

In what my client describes as a miracle, within ten days they received a full price offer. We were all surprised and joyful. How did this happen? We merely allowed this property to be part of the universal energy field and we fed it a positive frequency. Rather than being a financial anchor that was haunting my client and creating problems, we transcended the energy. The real joy came immediately when my client agreed to let go of the (financial) death sentence they had given themselves regarding this matter. The moment they changed their perception, energy, and outlook about this, their life changed for the positive. Would the buyer still have made an offer if my clients didn't transcend their energy? Probably, but it doesn't matter. What mattered was the relief my clients felt when they changed their perspective and how it affected their life. Instead of fear, worry and overwhelm, they chose to let go, stay positive and release their attachment to negative results.

Did the energy we created sell the property? Yes! The negative, problem-infested thoughts, words, and feelings my client had been experiencing were blocking the property from being sold. Even if the property had not sold in the next week, my client was thrilled to gain a new perspective that was helpful, peaceful and loving. The negative perception my client had when I spoke to them the first time about the property was destroying their entire life. We eliminated their negative attitude and committed to having a positive result, no matter what happened. Negative thoughts do not produce positive results.

Are the results that my clients got in the example above going to happen every time? No! Not if we are speaking about the final sales price. Selling the property for the highest amount possible wasn't our focus; we were detaching and creating an energy that would attract the perfect buyer for this property. I didn't mention that they actually had three properties they were selling and all of the properties sold within a month. Once my clients changed their perception and energy about their investment properties, they stopped blocking the sale of the properties.

I believe that many of you can relate to this situation or one similar to it because we all have challenges in our lives. First, we acknowledged how many problems there have been based on the actual events, we acknowledged the fear they felt and then we looked at how we could immediately improve their situation. We made a list of what actions to take to improve the energy of the overall situation. We determined what the best next action item was and focused on infusing that with authentic Divine energy. It made the difference! How we feel inside is far more critical than what is happening in the physical world. We can influence any intention we have by transcending energy. We may not get the results we were hoping for, but we will have a peaceful, loving experience that will improve our life. Ultimately the results are not as important as the energetic vibration we are creating to support our intention.

Are you in support of your life purpose or are you in resistance to it? You have guideposts available to you that will show you if you are remaining connected to the universal flow of energy. The easiest way to determine if you are on track is to recognize when you are not generating energy that supports your life purpose. This is when awareness becomes critical. You have so many beliefs and obligations in your life that don't support who you are today. The simplest thing to do is to examine some of your stories and beliefs and see how they are affecting your life. Are they blocking you or supporting you? Once you have an understanding and start to gain awareness of your inner beliefs that might be blocking you, stopping you or holding you back, you can make a different choice. Our challenges are all created by the past experiences of life and are supported by the stories we have created which we tend to protect.

Imagine for a moment that you're sitting in the forest next to a beautiful stream of crystal clear mountain water. There is a boulder in the middle of the stream and the waters flowing down bounces off the boulder and continue flowing down stream. The boulder is in constant resistance to the stream and flow of water. The stream flows and the boulder sits oblivious to the flow of the stream. Are you a boulder, in resistance, blocking the flow universal energy? Eventually, something has to give in when there is constant resistance. Resistance creates struggle and struggle creates a need to protect what you believe is right. It is a constant battle that eventually gets the best of you in some form. What will it be? Your finances? Perhaps your health or your relationships?

The one constant in life is change, and there are billions of changes occurring in and around our lives every moment of every day. The universe is energy in motion, it is always expanding, always changing because the

energy is continuously intersecting with other energies and creating manifestations. Why not get in touch with how the flow of universal energy
moves? Floating downstream is more comfortable than standing in the middle of the stream, or worse, trying to swim upstream. Which way do you
experience life? It may be best to get another person's opinion on this question because you may not be capable of answering these questions honestly.
When you go to the source of the problem to get the answer, you will be
listening to rationalized logic. Your ego invests a lot of time in maintaining
control of your life and is always prepared to answer these questions with
well-rehearsed rationalizations. Getting an outside opinion is often best.
Who would you ask? As you think about people to ask, consider which
person's opinion raises fear in you more than any other? That might be the
best person to ask!

When you live in survival, your focus is on rationalizing your misery and finding relief, a way to be happy. Your understanding of the information that resides in you causes a desire to defend your reality and perceptions
of life. Understanding how you are doing this will set you free. If there are
stories that you continue to protect you will continue to block yourself from
your Divinity. Typically people have stories that revolve around survival and
lack which are centered directly in fear. Lack is a belief system that there is
not going to be enough to go around, so you better get what you can now.
Lack takes shortcuts and always looking for a "cheaper" way. Lack drives

fast because there isn't enough time for everything, and tries to do too much at once. The list about lack goes on and is always about "Not Enough" (time, money, food, etc.).

People who live in lack are typically incapable of receiving because they don't know how to hold an abundant space that is open to receiving. They may feel that it is wrong for them to receive something if they are not giving something back. Sometimes it is because they give to others with a "string" attached, hoping for the desired outcome from their acts of giving. That is not giving; it is taking! I had a real struggle with receiving due to my lack of self worth. Having an abundant perception allows us to give and receive without any attachment, only from a loving space. Survival breeds lack.

The worst perception we hold is our need to defend ourselves. Notice what causes you to be defensive. No, I am not talking about a situation where you may be physically harmed. I am referring to the need to defend your beliefs and stories every day. If you listen carefully, people are speaking from a defensive perception in most conversations every day. It isn't what is said that is important, it is the inner belief that is creating the understanding, response and energy. Our outward expressions (words and physical reactions) will always speak to our inner beliefs. We use rationalizations and justifications to defend our life of survival because a competitive mindset is required. Our focus remains on living at a higher comfort level in our life of survival. Survival demands competition. There is always going to be a winner and a loser!

When you look at life in the simplest form, it is based on either Love or Fear. Everything you do in life comes from one of these two places. I know that before starting my transformation, my entire life was fear based. Everything I did in life was based on the amount of fear I felt, my immediate reaction to it and what I needed to do to survive. I was in a constant state of fear. Now I realize that when I come from a perspective of love, I will improve the situation for all involved. Just having this awareness allows me the opportunity to choose and be responsible for my choice. If you look at life only from this perspective, it will change your life quickly because love and fear cannot co-exist. Many years ago I heard a saying that I still repeat today, "Fear knocked on the door and love answered, but no one was there"! You only need to use fear and love as your guideposts. Always choose love, it will support your intentions and deliver results that are beyond your current ability to comprehend. Defensiveness is completely fear based and is all about how your survival (physical life) will be affected. Love needs no defense! In fact, the most important thing you can do with love is to give it away. There is nothing to defend when we speak from love and the more love you share, the more you will receive.

Guideposts for Your Journey.

1. When you respond to others with negative thoughts, words or actions, what causes you to respond in this manner.

2. Identify two stories that you have that no longer serve you and block you from your potential.

3. Write about an experience you had where transcendence changed the energy of the situation and the outcome.

CHAPTER SIX ~ The Best Things in Life Aren't Things

Trust is the secret ingredient that has allowed me to experience freedom. I didn't trust myself or my logic before, because my motivations had always been fueled by expectations. I have since found that my results are better when I let the universal vibration determine the outcome. I learned to trust the universe by observing my energy. As I stepped back from my emotions, it allowed me to look at any situation in life objectively. I observed what happened and asked how I could improve it by providing supportive energy. This approach reduced my involvement significantly and provided me with a lot more free time to do other things. In the past, I was attached to the chaos, and I reacted from a perspective of survival with a need to protect myself. Or maybe I saw an opportunity to get someone's approval by taking care of the problem or taking care of them. I took action even when I didn't need to be involved because of my survival instincts. I didn't know how to trust myself or anyone else; trust is not a tool used for survival. When I accessed universal energy, I was required to trust implicitly.

Universal energy is invisible, non-physical, and it's always in motion expanding organically, like vibrations attracting like vibrations and coming together in a constant state of expansion. You get to see the results of this every day in your life. Sometimes it catches you by surprise like thinking of someone you haven't seen in quite some time, and then seeing them, or they call shortly after. Have you ever had an experience where you meet someone, and your energies are overwhelmingly attractive to both of you, and you become quick friends? These are examples of energy in motion and the proof is how you felt when it happened. Typically this is only called a coincidence because it defies an explanation from a physical perspective. It is energy in motion connecting in the non-physical and manifesting into physical form. As I learned about manifesting, I immediately realized it required me to create positive energy, let go of any attachment to the outcome and trust!

When I look back at the experiences in my life, I remember them based on how they made me feel. The most memorable moments are the ones that created an authentic connection, a special feeling, maybe re-connecting with a loved one or having an intimate conversation with someone special. The best things in life will always have to do with how they made me feel. I was involved in the making of a Wisdom Film with Bob Proctor; it's called "A Marvelous Power. In the wisdom film, Bob Proctor said something very profound that I will never forget. "The day we die everything we own will go to someone else, but everything we are will stay with us forever."

Bob was referring to the non-physical qualities that make up our "chi" or life force. We can accumulate wealth in the material world, but it will never satisfy the inner craving for personal fulfillment. The only thing that is going to fulfill our desire for authentic self-expression, self-actualization and living our true life purpose is the ability to connect with and understand the non-physical resources that are available to us. What happens in our physical reality is always influenced by the non-physical energy we feed into our physical reality. The more familiar we are with these energies, the more powerful we become.

I like to keep life simple. I am always looking for guideposts that are very easy to see so I know I am on the right path. As I focused on the non-physical, I realized that my focus is always on what's next in my day, remembering that remaining present will enhance my results. When I am present, my focus is on the energy that is fueling my words and actions. When I am operating unconsciously, my mind is someplace other than where I am at physically. I am quite sure that you can think of many different instances when your attention was someplace other where you were at the time. Your energy is also going to be some other place; where your mind goes your energy flows. Each day I see many instances where I could have been more present. You will always have many disruptions happening in your life. It is your response to them, and how they affect you emotionally, that determines your ability to remain present. One of the characteristics of living a self-actualized life is learning to be selfless rather than selfish. When you aren't present, you are consumed by your thoughts and that limits your ability to be consciously present allowing you to be selfless.

It isn't the events taking place in our world that cause trouble; it is our response to the events in our life that determines our energy. The universe is perfect; it is our perception of it that is out of balance. There is a higher Divine Order that orchestrates the universe, and we have access to this energy if we choose. When we get consumed with survival, we are always going to be focused on material things and the physical world. When we are focused on the non-physical we are no longer surviving, we are thriving and focused on expansion in every area of our life. When choosing to connect with the thriving selfless energy as often as possible, we realize that we are part of an overall universal plan. When we choose to participate in the Universal plan, we only need to focus on the energy flowing through us. The clarity of our intention determines the speed of the universe's response to our energetic vibration. Remaining present allows us to gain more clarity and increase our energy, allowing our vibration to determine what we are going to attract into our life.

"Fear knocked on the door, and love answered... but no one was there!."

— *Author Unknown*

It is the non-physical where all of our power resides. Our ability to transmit energy that will create the best solution for everyone, in any situation, is real power! What is happening in the physical isn't as important as how we respond to it energetically. We live our lives based on our internal beliefs which are supported by the stories we have buried deep inside, some of which we never care to visit again. These stories were developed to protect us, and when we start unraveling the stories, we can easily see that they don't support us any longer. Each time you're triggered, dig a little deeper and gain more awareness. You will notice how the negative energy from your stories start to diminish and more solutions start to appear. The universe always responds to your request; the universe always answers if you are patient.

Our potential resides in the non-physical world. Our true potential sits right on the other side of our challenges, blocks and life lessons. It's all about the inner game; what's going on inside of us. When we start to unravel all of the stories inside us we will notice a significant difference in how we feel and our physical results. This is our access to our authentic self-expression, looking at life from a physical and a non-physical perspective. The physical is everything physical in our life, anything that is outside our skin. When we maintain an outlook from the non-physical, our feelings (heart energy) are allowing us to access our true power and flow our authentic self-expression.

There are simple guidelines to follow which will allow you to gain more awareness of how to support your energy. They indicate whether or not your focus is on the physical or the non-physical. You will quickly understand the difference between these perspectives as you apply these simple guidelines. You will notice that none of these examples define what is happening in the physical, only how you perceive the events in your life.

The place to begin is with Fear and Love.

Fear is the most common feeling known because it is the cornerstone of a survival-based lifestyle. Fear is a good thing! It tells us when we need to make conscious choices from our heart. When we respond to fear from our "head" our ego wants to protect us. Based on our past experiences and our internal belief system, fear will generate a negative response to any situation. It is so powerful that it immediately creates a fight or flight response. Fear gets our attention and our egos use this tool wisely to maintain control of our lives. Fear is "False Evidence Appearing Real." Fear always wants to know how we are going to do anything and blocks us from moving forward. This is not fear as it is related to a life-threatening situation, rather it is free-floating fear generated from internal beliefs. Fear creates perceptions of conflict, loss, not being good enough, and worrying what others will think. It is the energy of protection, procrastination, lack of self-worth, manipulation and control.

Will you be able to get rid of (eliminate) your fear? No! Fear is an intrinsic part of the human learning experience. It shows you what direction to go to or what to stay away from based on your choices. When you face your fears, you gain power, you clear your path, and you stop wasting your energy worrying. Each choice to step through fear creates a big shift in your energetic momentum. It is your awareness of your fears that will allow you to make choices that truly support your life purpose. Fear is telling you that you are facing the unknown and your imagination has already created an adverse scenario in your head. When you experience fear and choose not to face it, the fear will be running your life. Notice anytime you are encountering fear, the source of the fear is going to be something in your physical reality. If we respond to fear with love, the fear dissipates and the answers will appear. This is when miracles will start happening. The more love you give, the more you get! Love is the energy that overpowers everything. When you share a loving perspective, it gets received in the exact manner you share it. Even if the person on the other end of your giving doesn't respond lovingly, your love will be accepted.

"Common sense is nothing more than a deposit of prejudices laid down in the mind before you reach eighteen."

— *Albert Einstein*

If you used the guideline of "Love or Fear" before you take any action, your life would improve significantly. Are you responding to fear with fear or making a conscious choice? Love and fear cannot co-exist, and when you come from a place of love, the fear dissipates.

Are you living in Limitation or Expansion?

We live in a self-policing society; anyone who is operating out of the "normal" is typically going to get challenged. The physical world is about limitation, and the non-physical world is about expansion. If we want to accomplish big things in life, we are likely to encounter resistance or feedback that isn't supportive. It is essential for people living in survival to maintain rationalizations that justify their quality (or lack of quality) of life. We make up stories in our head to compensate for all of the shortcomings we experience in life. We have been taught to work hard, live within our means and not upset the apple cart. We have been given these obligations from family, friends, and others that they expect us to fulfill. In many cases, these obligations don't support who we are today and keeps us in limitation.

Limitation is a state of restriction and expansion is infinite abundance. When you examine the universal laws, you will realize that they only support expansion. When we use the Universal resources, we only need an idea and the energy to support its growth. That's it, nothing else is required! The universe just works with energy; everything is a vibration, and everything comes from nothing! What is expansion? If you can imagine it, you can generate the energy to create it! When you connect to the universe with intention and energy, you will quickly understand that the universe provides all the tools you need to create anything you desire. The universe can't say no, but the universe does need to know. It is your intentions and energy that are going to allow the universe to know, and once you have created a safe foundation for your intentions, they are delivered.

The universe is a vibration. It is always moving and always changing in a constant state of organic growth, like energies that are attracted by energies of a similar vibration, and they merge to deliver a physical result. If you don't like the result, change your energy. If the universe didn't deliver your desire, you need more clarity about the essence of your intention. The universe only wants to deliver; it is your job to create the message to the universe through your energy and support it with your choices each day. Are you generating energy that is surviving or thriving?

Do you stay attached to the known or like to explore the unknown?

Survival is a life well known! It demands that we do not take risks, protect what we have, avoid any loss and stay safe. Even though our environment is not as abundant as we desire, we continue to make choices that support survival when we choose from fear, lack, not being good enough and concern for what others might say. It may not be the best place in the world, but it's familiar and feels safe to us.

I am developing a way to get my message out to more people that want to live their life purpose. I have a great business with clients from all around the world, a nice income and beautiful home. And all of these things are getting in the way of significantly growing my business to a much larger level. I am comfortable and have a fear of the unknown because I intend to increase my activity significantly. It requires stopping how I do business now and committing 100% to my new plan. No question that the unknown creates fear, and I know the path to growth and expansion is walking through the fear. If I always do what I have always done, I will get the same results. Venturing into the unknown is where our personal and business growth, potential, and personal fulfillment awaits us. I always look for the unknown; that is where your untapped-potential sits. The unknown areas of your life typically sit right behind your fear. Fear is an integral part of life, it is not going to go away, and it serves a valuable purpose in your life. Learn to love your fear, face your fear, and step into your fear and experience massive growth. Fear is a guidepost that takes you directly into your potential.

The Difference Between Your Head and Your Heart.

When you are trying to understand the difference between the physical and the non-physical, using your head vs. heart is a reliable guideline to know when you are living a life of survival. When you are in your head, you are in survival. When you ask your heart for the answer, you are going to thrive.

Earlier in the book, I spoke about the importance of being present in each moment so you can create energies that support your intentions.

This is why the head and the heart are firm guideposts that delineate between the physical and the non-physical. It is impossible for you to be present when you are in your "head" (mind). Your brain is only capable of regurgitating past experiences; your mind is not capable of being present because it can only reference the past. When you reference the past, you are generating the energy of your self-limiting beliefs; an energy that is not going to support your growth today. It will only encourage limitation. Ask your heart; it holds the answer.

I love what Eckhart Tolle taught us in his book "A New Earth." The most significant lesson I received from this book was understanding how we create problems. The only way to create a real problem is to re-live your past; we don't have problems in the present moment! When we are present with anyone else, connecting through our hearts, we are creating loving energy. Loving energy is always going to support our intention or desire in life. We are in a state of expansion when we are sharing loving energy. We are typically in our mind(s) while connecting with another person, we are more focused on how we are going to answer instead of being actively involved in the conversation. "What's in it for me" is the battle cry of a survival lifestyle! What Eckhart Tolle taught me is that to have a problem I must leave the present moment and go to the past or into the future. In this moment, right now, we have no problems!

Being present with loving energy means that you are connected, and you know that everything you give gets returned to you many times over. The energy of love is only about the giving and receiving. If you are not open to receiving love you cannot share it because love is not a one-way street; it is a two-way street and receiving love is just as important as giving it. You are capable of sharing love with others in direct proportion to the amount of love you hold for yourself. You can't share what you don't have, and when you attempt this it is not going to be authentic. You "feel" the difference when authentic self-expression is not present. Love is non-physical, and when shared with others it is given freely with no strings attached; this is unconditional love. Romantic love is not unconditional love; romantic love is more about the physical aspects of love to satisfy your basic physical needs. There is a great deal of physical attachment to romantic love, the person, the experience, the sex and two people joining together to make survival easier. You have feelings for the other person, but you also have expectations for the relationship to satisfy your physical needs. This is one reason many marriages fail, one partner has external expectations that the other person is no longer fulfilling. When your happiness is determined by fulfilling physical desires "outside" of you, you are not able to focus on creating an intimate relationship.

Now let's look at the difference between power and force.

Power is non-physical, while force is a physical trait. Force is the strength and vitality required for sustained physical or mental activity. Force is using your focus and commitment to achieve an outcome (expectation). When force is in play, you will typically see an expectation that someone is committed to and they are going to apply all of their abilities, energy and strength to achieve the expectation. The problem with force is the wreckage created on the path to fulfilling your expectation. When you have a survival mindset you are out to win, it's competitive, and there must be a winner and a loser. This is how I was living life; forcefully trying to survive at a higher level but that is not what you saw when we spoke. I maintained my "happy face" facade on the outside while I was scheming to find a way for you to fulfill my expectation. When you are living in force there is no flow, only go! You'll keep taking actions until you get the desired results, with no regard for anything except winning. Force is all about your expectation. Force is always going to encounter resistance.

Connecting to the most powerful resources available to us and allowing them to flow through our lives while we are in service to others is authentic power. Authentic power is generated through our hearts to be shared with one and all, for the benefit of one and all. When we connect with others through our hearts, we are beginning to experience our life purpose and our connection with authentic power. I have been teaching authentic power to CEO's and business owners for the past five years, and the results have been miraculous. Once my clients understand the difference between power and force and how energy works, they start applying it in their life and they are always amazed at the results, It is simpler, easier, less time consuming and it feels wonderful. Authentic self-expression and authentic connection are filtering more and more into business, not only in the corporate culture, but it is also starting to be a requirement of customers. They only want to spend their money on products that are backed up by authenticity.

When you connect with someone authentically you are acknowledging that you are equal, you come from love and your motivation is the best outcome for all involved. This is Authentic Power, creating collaboration rather than competition.

Accountability and responsibility, which do you think is physical and which is non-physical?

By definition, a person that is accountable is required or expected to justify actions and decisions to the person in charge. In other words, you have an obligation that is being measured (judged) by someone else. Accountability is entirely physical because it involves answering to someone or something in the material world. Whatever you are accountable for is an obligation and the anticipated physical results or expectations have been predetermined by someone else. I speak about this in my coaching every day; I am a responsibility coach. When you have an accountability coach everyone's eyes are on the target or goal, which is going to be a physical result achieved.

The coach takes a client through a series of exercises that are intended to allow their client to reach their goal. The focus is on the physical actions; what are they doing? What are the results they achieved doing that? What do they need to do to get a better result? The focus is fixed on improving the client's level of survival because the goal is always an external material expectation.

We wonder why it's so difficult to achieve our goals or why we never start! Accountability creates an uphill battle that generates resistance, stress and a strong possibility that we will use manipulation to get the desired results (physical expectation) and get the approval of the person to whom we are accountable. Accountability creates obligations, and we tend to allow these obligations to control our lives. The commitments I am referring to are obligations that are imposed on us by others, and they are either spoken or assumed. We have been taught very well to behave in a manner that will please others as an obligation that gets approved or rejected by someone else. Many of the stories that we protect buried deep inside of us are obligations we feel toward those we love. Is this a problem? Yes! We are living by beliefs that are imposed upon us and may not serve our evolution today. I have found many different unspoken obligations that I took on, and most of them occurred in my childhood. We are accustomed to being controlled by someone else's standards, beliefs, and physical desires. A self-actualized person realizes that when choosing to do something for another person, they are choosing to commit, and are responsibly obligated to the result.

Responsibility is making a conscious commitment to take actions, measure results, share transparently and make adjustments moving forward with gratitude and love knowing the results are going to be perfect. My clients love my responsibility coaching because they have never had the opportunity to participate in life with a responsibility mindset. Our lives have been built on accountability to others since the day we were born. When clients see the puzzle pieces start to come together they realize immediately that viewing life from a perspective of responsibility is exciting, full of unlimited potential and a catalyst that will allow them to live a self-fulfilled life.

"The highest form of ignorance is when you reject something you don't know anything about."

— *Wayne Dyer*

Your mission is to develop a blueprint for your life and find anything in your life that doesn't support your path to your life purpose. The moment you learn about the non-physical resources available and gain awareness of the internal beliefs inside of you that don't support them, your life changes immediately. When you can be authentically responsible for your life, you will have control of your life path. Ultimately, awareness is what I teach. I am showing you all of the resources available to live a fully conscious and responsible life that takes you directly to your life purpose. You must choose to access the resources and use them.

I don't have a system or process because systems and processes are developed to control your actions and take you to a pre-determined result. Systems are physical, and I teach how to use powerful non-physical resources. When you are working with a system, they are typically one-size-fits-all! Each of you is unique; your differences are defined by your inner beliefs and your chi (life force energy). Giving everyone the same system and steps to follow would ignore your uniqueness.

When we acknowledge each person's uniqueness, we are empowering them to share themselves authentically.

That is the power of allowing others to be responsible instead of accountable. You know what to do with the non-physical resources once you learn what they are and how they function. As you create awareness of the universal resources, you will have a multitude of choice in any situation. You control your life, and you get to choose how much responsibility you want in your life. You get to choose what will serve you best. Your responsibility is to create an internal foundation, through your thoughts, words, and actions that demonstrate to the universe that you are ready for a higher level of responsibility. The universe allows you to have as much responsibility as you desire and all of the miracles, abundance, peacefulness, joy, and love that comes with that level of responsibility.

Defensiveness and Open-mindedness

When I decided to change my life I knew that I had to examine every aspect of my life. I quickly learned that I was living defensively, always ready to protect myself, my beliefs and the stories that support those beliefs. "You don't understand", is the battle cry a defensive person. When I was defensive, I was always looking for approval, and I was very defensive! I was defending the thoughts, actions, and behaviors that were creating all of my misery! I was shocked to see how I spent a majority of my time defending myself. No one was attacking me; I had learned defensiveness through my struggle with low self-esteem.

When we have a survival mindset we use defensiveness to protect ourselves, our families, our lifestyle and our beliefs. It boils down very quickly to a need to be "right." When we are defensive, it is common to measure our convictions against others and make judgments regarding their beliefs in comparison to ours. We are always measuring either better than or less than the person we are measuring. As we hear another person state their different opinions, which are different than our beliefs, we start to develop our defense immediately (either how to respond or how to exit). We are too busy thinking about how we will respond to what someone is saying, rather than being present in the conversation. Our fight or flight warning signals sound, and we step deeper into survival to protect our beliefs. Why do we protect them? Because if the other person is right, we must be wrong.

Defensiveness places us in a state of continuous resistance. We have our heels dug in, and we are holding our position. Defensiveness creates dis-ease. When we examine the physical aspects of being defensive, we will see that defensiveness creates extreme limitation. When we focus our effort on protecting something, there is no opportunity for growth; it keeps us stuck, in one place defending our belief.

"The human emotional system can be broken down into roughly two elements: fear and love.
Love is of the Soul, Fear is of the Personality."

— *Gary Zukav, "The Seat of the Soul"*

Open-mindedness is the key requirement for living a self-actualized life. We must blaze a new trail if we want to make changes. Having these guideposts that will steer us towards self-actualization and our true life pur-pose makes the path easier to follow as we step into the unknown. We can't find self-actualization based in the physical world; it requires a journey into our "inner-game" and the non-physical. Sometimes it is difficult to know if we are choosing what is best for our evolution, our heart will guide us directly to self-actualization; we need only learn to listen to our heart and understand our feelings. Open-mindedness is the acknowledgment that ev-eryone is on their journey, and we each have our perception of our journey in life. We are all equal. No one is more spiritual, more self-actualized or better than anyone else.

It is from the spirit of open-mindedness, reverence, and respect that I view everyone else's spiritual journey. Other people have the right to be themselves, and I am here to support them as they learn to live their true life purpose. Each of us is on a journey through life and depending on what is happening in another person's life, they will have their perception and opinions, and this is their statement of where they are on their spiritual journey.

We are all on a spiritual journey; we are not here to accumulate a bunch of "stuff," we have come to heal our souls.

Do You Know the Difference Between Intention and Attention?

We are accustomed to being told to "pay attention," as we have heard this throughout our childhood and maybe even today as adults. Attention has a physical perspective because we are focused outside of ourselves on an object, goal or something in the material world. Understanding attention is a wonderful guidepost to use as we are activating our self-actualization and starting to live our true life purpose. Where our attention goes, we go! I am not referring to paying attention so we can learn something. We tend to focus our attention out in the future, to achieve a goal, a vacation, a trip or getting a physical desire fulfilled. The problem is that attention captures us and we are unable to remain present to what we are doing in the present moment. When our attention is on a goal, our actions will support obtaining the goal which is something in the physical.

The intention is non-physical. When you have an intention, it will be energized by your thoughts, words, and actions in each moment. As you allow yourself to fuel your intentions energetically, it requires that you stay present to what you are doing. Whatever you are doing at that moment can be transcended by the energies that you are using to manifest your intention. No matter what you are doing, this choice along with every other choice you make is either magnetizing or repelling your intention. How will it feel to have your intention fulfilled? You visualize your intention as the best possible result and feel the energy that it creates inside of you. After visualizing your intention to the best of your ability, keep focusing on the energy that was created when you are connected to your intention. Tell the universe you intend for results that meet or exceed your ability to visualize your intention. Do this for a few minutes each morning and connect to the energies of the manifestation of your intention and then allow that energy to flow through you all day. This will activate the manifestation, and when fulfilled it will more than likely be better than anything you could have imagined!

Do You Understand Abundance or Do You Live in Lack?

I was raised in lack! I understand it now, but it took a long time to break away from a belief of lack. My parents grew up during the depression (1929-1939). I can't imagine what life was like at that time, but I know how it affected my upbringing. Here are some examples; shut the refrigerator door, turn off the lights when you leave a room, don't take such a long shower, and the list goes on and on. These are things that I learned as a child and still affect me today, and at times I must stop and make sure that I am choosing from abundance, not lack. I have an internal belief that always heads me directly to lack; get it cheaper, make it last longer, get more for less is always a perception of there not being enough. Lack smothers abundance, and there is plentiful abundance of everything in the universe. In the physical world of limitation, we can easily get trapped into the beliefs that support lack. This isn't about living conservatively, making responsible choices and spending money wisely. Lack is the belief that supports not having enough of anything. When we live with that energy, we will only be able to see and create shortages because that is what our belief is supporting.

Lack is the opposite of abundance. Everyone that I have coached did not understand abundance, and you may not know also. When I ask about abundance, everyone responds intellectually (from the head), and everyone thinks abundance means money and personal wealth. Abundance gets created in your heart, and the energy of abundance is giving, loving, sharing and knowing that there is an infinite abundance of everything for everyone. When abundance is understood, you flourish abundantly in all areas of your life. Abundance isn't money! Abundance is everything that attracts money to you energetically; abundance is a money magnet! Abundance applies to everything in life and life is plentiful.

Are you questioning or doubting any of these statements in your mind? Right now a survival mindset is going to start going into reaction because it can't comprehend infinite abundance. What is it that you are having a problem accepting? Follow that belief back to the story that supports it; now you are at the source of your struggles. Change your internal stories, and you change your life. Are you challenged with there not being enough time in the day? There is never enough time and too many things to do and not enough time to do them. These are characteristics of survival, lack, and absence of trust. Time abundance will be viewed as a gift beyond measure. When you have all the time in the world for authentic connections and the expression of your true life purpose. You will learn that there are many different forms of abundance. Abundance is a plentifulness of all the authentic parts of life. Abundance and gratitude go hand in hand; you can't have abundance without gratitude. As you go through your day, today, look at everything with an abundant perspective and ask yourself if you feel grateful, regardless of your current situation.

This is so simple, and you too easily make it so complicated. Are you living from the inside or is life-based on all the physical material things that are outside of you? Are you asking your head for the answer or listening to your heart? Once you grasp the concept of the physical and the non-physical you have a reliable guidepost that will guide you directly to transcendence.

Thriving requires collaboration with the universe and to receive the highest level of support from the universe; you must understand the operating instructions. Remember that the universe holds an infinite amount of potential and when you flow energy from the non-physical into the physical, you are creating a magnet for your intentions and dreams. Stay out of the results because expectations severely limit your results. Universal non-physical resources will deliver based on your energetic support and the results many times are well beyond anything you could imagine.

Get out of the way! You are a spiritual being; you are not a spiritual doing! That is your mission; learn to get out of the way and allow the power of the universe to manifest your most intimate and cherished intentions and desires. Staying connected energetically allows you to access the purest form of wisdom and energy the universe has to offer. I still have trouble getting out of the way because my ego always wants control. This requires consciousness, and the state of being presently aware in the moment strengthens my authentic connection. The journey is what makes life a grand adventure, not the destination. Your destination is death; this is inevitable. Are you focused on what you can accumulate or how you can make an authentic difference in the world? Start today with transitioning your life to the authentic energy that you are here to share with the world; it's never too late to start. Join the miraculous splendor of the universal flow of energy as it flows through your life, after all, you are a very important part of the universe. It is a simple way to live that yields magical results.

Guideposts for Your Journey.

1. Do you understand how to identify the different ways you focus on the physical results and how to support your life with non-physical energy? Identify which words below are physical or non-physical perspectives.

Head/Mind - Heart

The Unknown - The Known

Expansion - Limitation

Fear - Love

2. Are you defensive? List one way that you automatically respond defensively and one possible way you could respond rather than being defensive. How is this defensiveness blocking you now?

3. Practice breathing in love. Sit quietly, with your eyes closed and take a deep breath in filling yourself with love. When you exhale, allow your fear to leave. As you breathe in love, notice how you feel. This is the energy that you want to fuel your thoughts, words, and actions.

7) https://www.youtube.com/watch?v=0Pbj5bhvCt0

CHAPTER SEVEN ~ Living Abundantly

As I continue to uncover more secrets to living a self-fulfilling life, I continue to see results that support my teachings. The answer to life's biggest question is flowing the energy of your Divine Gifts into life and expressing yourself authentically while in service to others. The two essential ingredients are gratitude and abundance. What you desire most is your authentic self-expression, for that is the missing piece that creates self-fulfillment. Your authentic self-expression is your thoughts, words and actions infused with the energy of your Divine Gifts.

Don't change your life today. Simply allow yourself to start to become familiar with the resources that I have outlined in this book. As you learn more about these powerful resources, you will gradually transition to a life of thriving which is your natural state of being; it is your birth-right. You did not come to earth to learn survival and how to accumulate material wealth. You don't see any U-Haul trucks following the hearse to the cemetery so you can take your material accomplishments with you to the grave. Your objective is to create a legacy that is so powerful that it creates love, gratitude, and abundance for everyone you encounter in life. Your energetic expression of your Divinity can only create peace, love, joy, and abundance; there is no other outcome.

Free will and choice are the greatest gifts you have, and you learn to create a life of obligations that eliminates any possibility of free will and choice. You live with a perception that makes you believe you can't choose to live a more fulfilling life. The path to your life purpose is paved with free will and choice! You are free to choose anything you desire, and you are 100% responsible for the results created in your life. You typically end up with a perception that is opposite; your life is determined by decisions made by others. It is just a matter of perception and having no options indicates a life of survival. Are you willing to own your power and use it to share your unique gifts with the world? The more authentic spiritual responsibility you are willing to assume will allow you to live more powerfully. The greater your understanding of how being of service to others is your path to living a more powerful life, the faster you will grow. You are not here to be in servitude; you are here to be of service.

You live in two dimensions; the physical and the non-physical. To feel self-fulfilled, you must access the non-physical resources and infuse them into your life each day. Everything that is meaningful in life is being influenced by the power of non-physical energy. If you are attached to the physical results looking a certain way, that is an expectation, and you are in survival. When working with universal resources, there is no limit to what you can manifest. Your energy creates your perceptions. How you feel is going to determine what choices you make and actions you take. Transcendence allows you to nurture your intentions with loving, supportive energy and leave the physical results up to the universe. Living with a non-physical perspective enables you to be conscious of the energy you are generating and transmitting. The most exciting part is you get to choose, you move at a pace that is suitable for you, and you can transcend and transform your life at the speed of "choice." Choice without action is just a thought.

"Let your alignment (with Well-Being) be first and foremost, and let everything else be secondary. And not only will you have an eternally joyous journey, but everything you have ever imagined will flow effortlessly into your experience."

— Esther Hicks

We probably have spent decades protecting ourselves with stories, rationalizations, and justifications. It may take some time to penetrate those defenses. Having an open mind and the willingness to learn is all that is required. The moment that you choose to live a self-actualized life the universe will start providing you with opportunities to create more awareness. You will learn about the feelings inside you that are blocking you or standing in your way of living your true life purpose. It is an "inside job," and your feelings tell you instantly if you are moving towards a higher level of spiritual responsibility or remaining stuck in physical survival. Learning the truth about your shortcomings and acknowledging and loving them will cause them to diminish in strength, and over time your old beliefs, stories, and resentments will wither away.

Living your life purpose creates limitless possibilities and potential in your life. Clarity is vital because it is easy to get distracted by all of the infinite possibilities you'll encounter. A willingness to embrace the unknown in each moment with gratitude allows you to face any situation with a loving attitude focused on achieving the best result for all involved. The journey is more important than the destination; your journey is what is happening right here, right now. This is the journey. There is nothing in the world more satisfying than focusing on your journey because it allows you to feel self-fulfilled. The destinations you see in life are very elusive, but as you move towards your goal you gain more clarity, and you enhance your intention. The only destination you will reach in life is death. It is somewhat ironic that most people are focused on getting to death safely. They ignore their purpose, take on a survival mentality and focus on a higher level of comfort for their lifestyle.

Self-actualized people have respect and reverence for all that is known and unknown, realizing that everything is part of all that is in the universe, and they have access to everything the universe has to offer. The unknown holds their potential. This approach to life is unconventional because it is oblivious to their physical needs and focused on their personal growth and a desire to learn as much as possible about living their life purpose.

Having an understanding of the life lessons you're here to learn allows you to gain more awareness about your life. Awareness is a tool that will enable you to live a much more powerful life. You can observe what happens during the day and you'll see the same perception of your challenges appear again and again. Do you want to know who you are? Stop judging yourself! You are your own worst critic! Everything that makes your life miserable right now is the portal to the pathways that lead to your life purpose. It's important to learn as much as possible about the things that bother you because they will lead you directly to the belief that is not allowing you to feel self-fulfillment. The more awareness you gain about a belief that doesn't support you, the easier it is to change. You each have beliefs buried in your stories, and you allow your stories to create your life. Your stories aren't necessarily true but how you feel about them is true; your feelings speak only truth. Your stories shape your perceptions, and your stories are developed to protect you in a life of survival. It creates living in a constant state of defensiveness, safeguarding your shortcomings and making sure that you "fit in". This can only create an endless cycle of frustration, competition, and resistance-based struggle.

Ignoring the non-physical resources causes us to focus our attention on our physical desires. We will never be able to satisfy our material desires because everything in our physical world is temporary. Once we have obtained the material item we so desperately wanted, our happiness is short-lived, and our attention moves on to the next desire that we believe will make us happy. When buying a product with free will and choice, and gratitude as our foundation, we use different criteria to make our choice and appreciation is our response, not happiness. Everything in our life must support our intentions to live a meaningful life of purpose. We are not attached to how our life will look; we are creating how it will feel! There is nothing, absolutely nothing that feels better than living our true life purpose!

Intentions are focused on the essence of what you are creating, how it will feel when you experience the manifestation of your intention. Feelings are the language of the non-physical. The energy you use to attract your intention is heart-based feelings; this is the language of the non-physical. Manifesting powerfully occurs with your feelings, not your logic. Connecting to the essence of the experience you are creating accelerates your manifestation and the more clarity you have about the essence, the faster your manifestation appears. The word essence is defined in the dictionary as; spirit, nature, substance and a fundamental quality. What essential qualities of your life are enhancing your energy, perceptions, and manifestations? Support your intentions through the energy of the core essence of your intention and watch it manifest quickly.

When you are focused on your intentions, you develop a higher level of acceptance. Keep it simple, accept what is and make choices based on the essence of the intention and transcend your results to a higher energetic level. When you are only focused on the physical results, your only concern is creating and fulfilling your physical needs. Anything that appears contrary or in resistance to your desires creates a struggle, resistance and a need to control and manipulate life, so you get whatever you are chasing. You are unwilling to accept the results or the current influence that is blocking you from your desire. You find a way to blast through the block or work around it. When you are living your life purpose, you will realize that struggle, resistance and a desire to manipulate tell you that you're headed in the wrong direction. Using the resources I have shared and living your life purpose is like going on a permanent vacation! It makes life simple not complicated. It is much, much more strenuous, difficult and challenging not living your life purpose! Intentions allow you to attract people, places and things that are supportive of your life purpose. Clarity creates the power of our intentions.

Any time someone states their beliefs that are not in alignment with your intention, the universe is giving you an opportunity to own yourself. There is no need to "fit in," and when only given the "my way or the highway" option, a self-actualized person is headed to the highway! Self-actualized people do not want to be controlled by the auto-pilot mentality of society. Understanding free will and choice and pursuing your authentic self-expression is the most exciting journey you can take in life. When you choose to live your life purpose and state your intentions publicly to clarify your choices, you are claiming your authentic place in life. You are not defending your opinion; there is nothing to protect when you come from authentic love. When you are stating your position with love, it will be felt by all involved. If others speak or show disappointment in your choice, they are reacting to their expectations being threatened, even though they may be pointing the finger at you in judgment, blame, shame and guilt. You are not responsible for how others feel; you are only accountable for how you feel and the energy that you share with others.

We each have dharma (life purpose), and it is very exact. Everything in the universe has a purpose, and everything is connected energetically. Most people have already experienced living in their Divinity, if only for a moment. We have heard it referred to as "being in the zone" or having our "mojo" working. It is the times in our life that everything goes right and seems to keep getting better. It is exciting, almost shocking how simply everything happened. Then we get knocked out of the zone by a disruption in our life, and we are unable to find our way back. Due to the exact nature of our dharma, it is easy to get knocked off track. We are accustomed to making plans for the future with high expectations for our goals so that we can fulfill our desires. We are making plans for a future that we have no control over. Life is full of interruptions and disruptions, and with our attention on the future, it is impossible to stay present.

"Least effort is expended when our actions are motivated by love, because nature is held together by the energy of love."

— *Deepak Chopra, "The Seven Spiritual Laws of Success"*

Acknowledging our dharma and staying present allows fulfilling our life purpose at the moment without concern for the future. We have no control over our future as there are too many unknown external factors influencing the outcome. It is an exercise in futility that I have thoroughly tested while living in survival. It is much simpler to focus on the present moment because we can positively influence our future outcome. When we are living in the present moment, we can make instant course corrections energetically when our life is not meeting our intentions, energetically. This is transcendence, accepting our reality as it happens and transcending the energy to support the path that is aligned with our intentions and fulfills our life purpose.

As I started my transformation process, I felt like I was walking down a stepping stone path with my intentions through a minefield. As long as I stepped from one stone to the next my life was peaceful, but if I missed a stepping stone, boom! I got knocked off my path, and I felt like the forces were against me. That is how it felt because of the fear and chaos that I was familiar with in my life. It took time for the chaos to quiet down but it did come to an end. Chaos needs participants and when you eliminate yourself as a participant chaos always finds others that are willing to take your place. Chaos will not leave without having the last say, and it will be louder than normal; just like an infant that needs attention, your ego makes chaos screams louder!

My interactions with others while I was living a life of survival was typically very needy. I wanted to satisfy my physical needs and desires, and I wanted to know how they could help me because I didn't feel that I could do it on my own. This is how we get attached to others energetically and create a relationships that may not be supporting our life purpose today. These are energetic chords that still allow the other person to flow energy into our lives even though it doesn't support the expansion of our soul. A majority of these are created at a very young age, and we are afraid to cut the cord due to the potential repercussions from family or friends. We have always participated in this dance with other people, and they are going to notice when we choose to live our life purpose. Of course, the first thing that happens when the relationship changes is their ego telling them they aren't good enough and they were doing it wrong. How do we let them know that the relationship and chaos no longer support us? We do it with love, in the words we speak and tell them that we are making new choices and these choices have nothing to do with them; we are committed to living a self-fulfilled purposeful life. Remember, whatever we allow into our life is defining who we are physically and non-physically; it is a reflection us.

A client of mine told me that every week he called their mother to check on her and the conversation always turned negative. My client had a brother that was living life as a victim, and he blamed my client for all of his problems, yes every problem in his life! My client's mother spoke to both brothers often, and she always talked about her other miserable son when she talked to my client. My client's brother would not speak to him because he was too angry. This situation perpetuated itself for years and is still the same today, but not for my client. During one of the discussions with his mother, he explained how sad it was that this was destroying the family and he was not going to be responsible for his brother's misery and wasn't going to participate any longer in that conversation. He has transformed his relationship with his mother and thoroughly enjoys checking in with her now. There is nothing he can do about his brother except to love him from a distance and pray for him. Over time, love and prayers will be the victor.

As you make changes in your life, some abrupt and others more casually, you will create new relationships that are supportive of your commitment to live your life purpose. Current relationships will change, while not all relationships will remain intact, none will remain the same. You don't move to a new neighborhood and bring all of your old neighbors with you. You are changing your life, and it is going to affect everyone around you. Some will approve, and others will not approve because your relationship was based on the lifestyle you are changing. You are not responsible for anyone else's happiness other than yourself. As you continue to choose to live a self-actualized life, sharing your life purpose, you will see many of relationships change and will have a more authentic connection. Your transformation will be a reflection for others to witness how to live with true life purpose and live in peace, joy, and freedom. You are igniting new possibilities for others as you go through your day being transparent and sharing your loving energy.

One of the most challenging aspects of living your true life purpose is grasping the simplicity. You are probably accustomed to living in survival, and that is a complicated game that kept your mind very busy. The game never ends because you are always trying to create a different level of survival. Living authentically requires using your heart as your primary guidance system, as your heart knows the truth. Keep it simple, flow the energy of your Divine Gifts into your physical life. Take action fueled by non-physical resources and allow the universe to create the results. When you plant a garden, you provide water and other nutrients to your seedling, and over time it grows into a beautiful plant. You are doing the same with your life; nurturing and feeding supportive energy so you can blossom into your true life purpose and use your authentic self-expression to interact with the world. You know that others are living in survival and competing to win, and when there is a winner there also must be a loser. Some people will not be able to relate to you because their perception is so steeped in their fears. When you live in a competitive space you can only see others as winners or losers; there is no equality. When there is no equality, there is no authentic connection, only a stronger person taking advantage of a weaker person. That is the game of survival, competing to get everything you can get. When you rise above others' perceptions of life in survival, you create a new mirror for them to see a new reflection of your life purpose energy. Your energy is so powerful that you can transcend situations by just being present and not saying a word. That is authentic power.

The universal law of cause and effect is always operating in our lives, and our actions today determine our fate tomorrow. Karma gets created two ways: by the energy behind actions we take each day, and by the energy we produce when we are on the receiving end of cause and effect. We have the opportunity to learn how to generate energy to keep our karma in balance. We don't have any say about the disruptions in our life, they just happen, but we can control how we respond to these disruptions. We can transcend the energy at the moment if we become aware of the energy that is supportive of our intentions. If we don't transcend the energy, or at least establish the clarity that this is not energy that supports our life, we will automatically allow the energy to become part of our lives.

195

It is imperative that you create clarity in your life and make choices that support the life you are creating. Anything that shows up that doesn't fit your purpose you must address, transcend or disown, or it automatically becomes part of your energy. The more awareness you gain about yourself and your life is also giving you full awareness about other people in your life, and if they are supporting your journey. Having this knowledge allows you to view what is happening in your life with a much clearer perspective and you are no longer going to get "hooked in" to other people's problems, emotions, and neediness.

As you continue to grow, your energy becomes much more power-ful, and you do not tire as easily because you are not in a constant struggle to survive. You can continue to cleanse the toxins in your energy by mak-ing choices that support your Divinity. With each choice, you cleanse more, and you create more clarity and more power. You will notice a significant expansion of sensitivity in your intuition. Your intuition is a "feeling" or a "sensation" inside you that gets your attention. I call my intuitive messages "hits." I will be in the process of doing something and get a "hit" to call someone, go another direction or immediately share with another person the information I am getting. These "hits" are not thoughts but are accom-panied by a feeling, for me. This is when I need to trust and follow the guidance of the universal wisdom. Total trust is what it takes to follow my intuition. I am in constant contact with my energy, and I get many intuitive signals every day. It isn't a big deal, not to me, it is part of my authenticity and my connection with universal energy.

I was working with a client last year, and he was fascinated by intuition when I showed him what it was and how to connect with it. He shared a story with me that happened to him a few years ago. He had arranged for his family to get together in Thailand for the Christmas holidays and then visit Vietnam. His family lived in different parts of the world, and the trip was set up a year in advance. About 90 days before the trip he has a feeling they should change their itinerary, but he thought it was much too difficult because of all the different travel plans and reservations required. It bothered him so much that he called everyone and they moved the trip back one week, and because of this change they would go to Vietnam first. The week before they left, at the exact time they would have been in Thailand the tsunami hit Thailand! His entire family may have died because they were supposed to be where the tsunami hit. The way he explained it to me was that he "felt" as if he had no other choice, so he got everyone to agree to change the trip. This may seem like it is an extreme example, but it isn't because this is the way universal energy flows. It requires the ability to listen, and if your life is noisy, chaotic and busy, there may be too many physical distractions. When you stop the survival struggle and create time to be still and listen you automatically receive wisdom from the universe.

When there is less "chaotic noise" in your environment, you are more available to hear, sense or feel your intuitive guidance. The more you trust your "inner self" you will witness more miracles (coincidences) in your life, and life becomes meaningful, enjoyable and fulfilling. You get to participate at any level you choose. If you want to live life at the highest level, connect more with universal energy and universal wisdom. Allow your Divine Gifts to flow, take actions that support your Divinity, leave the results up to the universe and trust that results will be perfect. Perfection is in the eye of the beholder. When results measured by love are acceptable, but when you view results from a perspective of physical survival, something usually goes wrong, and you believe it could have been better. Observing life with gratitude and abundance changes the look and feel of everything you do in life. It is much simpler than you imagine. Follow the guidelines, learn to choose with more clarity and feed your intentions with as strong an energy as you can create.

"Authentic power is the real deal. You can't inherit it, buy it, or win it. You also can't lose it. You don't need to build your body, reputation, wealth or charisma to get it."

— *Gary Zukav*

Someone told me once that they were intimidated by spirituality because they didn't know the "lingo." I empathize with fear that creates a belief of that nature, but there is no special "lingo" in spirituality. There is no membership; this is our journey, and we get to choose our direction. There is mutual respect naturally displayed among individuals who are committed to spiritual growth, allowing each person to follow their truth. We are all at different places on our journey to universal truth, and we let each other have the experiences they choose individually. I may not agree with others' choices, but I respect their right to make what appears to be the best choice for themself. All paths lead to Divine Truth. It is our choice to determine how fast we progress on the path of truth. We all have different experiences, life lessons, and perceptions that will lead us to our authentic self-expression. Everything is different when we view life from the perspective of our Divinity. We are living in the physical world and using the non-physical guidelines to create a powerful, authentic and abundant life.

As you focus on your life lessons and healing yourself, you're creating a safer space for yourself. You'll feel more at peace, safer and more committed to having all of you and your authentic self-expression. Living in a safe area allows you to explore other unknown areas and you know you can safely return to your safe zone to process and get re-centered. There are many holistic practitioners teaching hundreds of different modalities that all explore the non-physical universe and can clear negative energy from your "inner game." Find some areas to explore or a unique path to follow that will allow you to discover more about yourself, someplace you've never been before. Notice how you feel as you go through these new experiences. What did you like, what did you not like and what feelings came up, when did fear appear? Choose something you do every day and find a new way to do it, explore new territory. If the path you are on looks familiar, go a different way. Take action without creating expectations for the outcome and allow the universe to deliver the rewards from the energy behind the choices and actions you take. It becomes a step-by-step process, and with each step, you will get to see the magnificence of the universe unfolding in front of you. This creates a desire to increase your energy, your power and your level of service to others. The only way to serve the world is with your unique Divine Gifts and flow your Divine energy into all of your actions. You will be teaching others to access their power through choice as they witness you manifesting the life of your dreams. Consider what reflection you are creating in the world.

Your relationship with the Divine continues to grow, but not by what you create in material form. Your growth reflects your level of peacefulness and abundance. As you gain new insights, you create a more powerful presence and more peace, joy, and love in your life. Start the journey slowly, be open, feel safe, be enthusiastic and passionate about your quest. It is an extraordinary journey that you can only take once. As you go deeper into your heart, you will know yourself on a more intimate level, and this will allow you to connect more authentically with other people. Each level of understanding brings new perceptions, language, and actions that enhance your life and the lives of those around you. Each inquiry into the unknown creates more awareness and a broader, safer spiritual path to travel. Be aware of your feelings and release them to cleanse away the powerful old emotions that are used to control our lives. As you feel these old emotions, you will notice how they are withering away. Your journey is one of constant searching, a continual process of uncovering old beliefs and feelings and taking new action to create new views that support your soul's expansion. Ideas you have today may not serve you tomorrow, as you are always in a state of expansion, creating new awareness and increasing your vibrational field.

Your Divinity is part of the flow of universal energy, and your Divine Energy must get expressed, you can't block the flow of Divine energy, it is always flowing. You have been preventing the energy from being used for its intended purpose. If you are not aware of your Divine Gifts and connected consciously with your Divinity, you are stuck in the physical. Don't struggle, relax and allow your energy to flow. You only need make a choice to allow it to flow, and it flows. The same is true for a river, it is always flowing like energy in motion. If the flow of the river is blocked, the water will build up until it overflows and causes chaos and destruction. Similar to the water in a river, our Divine Gift energy is flowing and when blocked, it will also cause destruction and chaos.

The path is yours to establish. You have your unique lessons to learn;

you get to choose which of the tools to work with and when to work with them. The choice is yours! This is the exciting part of the journey, having a path of transformation that you design, specifically for you. Move forward at your own pace and always remember that you are embarking on new actions and it is unfamiliar territory. It is only unfamiliar the first time, and then you gain more knowledge and awareness. With each experience you create more clarity, so be compassionate with yourself as you learn this new way of life and believe me when I say your life will always look new. There is always more to learn. If you knew how to do the new actions you are taking, you would already be living that way. Mistakes get made because you are learning new tools and resources, and you aren't going to do it perfectly! Give up perfection; it serves no purpose. Stay focused on your desire to learn as much as possible and live a more fulfilled life.

My experience on this path has been one of excitement and gratitude. I view it as a gift to have the desire to learn more about the true meaning of life. I don't have all the answers, and all of my resources are not the perfect answer, as there is no such thing. Waking up every morning with an inquisitive attitude about the universe and a burning desire to teach the information to anyone who has an interest is my greatest blessing. It is very humbling to teach this to another person and watch their life magically improve. Knowing that I am the conduit for this information to flow through, I maintain an attitude of reverence for the material, the manner in which it is received and the miraculous results it yields.

Life is simple if we remember that we are spiritual beings having a human experience. My desire for you is that you have identified one small piece of information in this book that you started applying and your life improved as a result. That is my intention and the intention for this book. My true life purpose is to empower others so they may empower others. Thank you for spending time with me, my beliefs and my teachings, I am grateful. I wish you blessings on your journey.

Guideposts for Your Journey.

1. What is one characteristic of self-actualization that you can focus on today to improve the quality of your life?

2. List three intentions that you are going to energize with your thoughts, words, and actions each day? How will you support these intentions and how will they improve your life?

3. Do you show others reverence and respect for their position on their spiritual journey?